The Golf
DELUSION

The Golf DELUSION

**Why 9 out of 10 golfers make
the same mistakes**

Lessons and stories from the
Knightsbridge Golf School
by
Steve Gould and D.J. Wilkinson

E&T

E&T

First published 2009 by Elliott and Thompson Limited
27 John Street, London WC1N 2BX
www.eandtbooks.com

ISBN 978-1-9040-2773-7

Pictures (studio and location) by Charles Briscoe-Wright (cbk.foto@zen.co.uk)
Pictures (pages 1, 36, 65, 71, 75, 81, 109, 143, 189, 191, 211): Getty Images
Picture (page 15): Popperfoto/Getty Images
Pictures (pages 33, 129): Augusta National/Getty Images
Pictures (pages 60, 111): Bob Thomas/Getty Images
Picture (page 72): Time & Life Pictures/Getty Images
Picture (page 181): AFP/Getty Images
Pictures (pages 100, 183, 192, 204): iStockphoto

Leslie King extracts taken from *The Master Key to Success at Golf*, 1961

Every effort has been made to trace copyright holders for images and
extracts used within this book. Where this has not been possible the
publisher will be happy to credit them in future editions.

9 8 7 6 5 4 3 2 1

A CIP catalogue record for this book is available from the British Library.

Printed in Italy by Printer Trento on sustainable paper.

Acknowledgements

We would like to thank:

Lorne Forsyth, Mark Searle, Ellen Marshall, Charles Briscoe-Knight,
Tina Bennett, Darrel Bennett, Andy Pharro, Dave Lamplough,
Ian Chapman, Hugh Grant, Anton Du Beke, Sir Christopher Lee, Bruce Forsyth,
Tony Lawrence, Roger Kean, James Collins, David Eldridge, Nicky Gyopari,
Natalia Kantovich, Hannah Comolli, Nick Price, Tom Birket, Eddie Cogle,
Diana Burlton, Miles Barr, Vernon Kay, Tom Cox and Ian Bloom.

CONTENTS

Foreword

No one in the world has had more golf lessons, or seen more teachers, than I have.

All I can say is that time and again, I come back to Steve and Dave and they always put me right. I truly believe that their obsession (inherited from Leslie King) with the early part of the backswing is indeed the key to a proper swing. When that part of my swing deteriorates, I have no chance. And when they've put it back in the groove I play at my best.

The same applies to countless friends I've sent to their basement, and to my aged father who has never been easy to teach.

This book is a brilliant distillation of their wisdom, and if you care about golf you would be insane not to read it.

Hugh Grant

PART ONE

THE GOLF DELUSION

Leslie King, the Knightsbridge Golf School and the Golf Delusion

Knightsbridge is one of the most prestigious locations in Europe. It is home to the rich and the famous, the socialites and the aristocrats and – surprisingly enough – to one of the most glamorous and successful golf schools in the world.

Located a mere Tiger drive away from Harrods and a short chip from the Harvey Nichols handbag display, a converted squash court beneath a Georgian façade may be the last place you would expect to see a golf lesson taking place. Yet it is our belief that, since its conception in 1951, more lessons have been given at the Knightsbridge Golf School than anywhere else on earth.

The School was founded by Leslie King, one of the first instructors to develop a system of teaching the golf swing. He never claimed to have invented a swing, but to have watched it and categorised it, pulling it apart to enable him to help

his pupils build a swing that was as near perfect as possible. He had devised his swing model from watching the great players of his day, building their swing fundamentals into a foolproof technique that could be learnt by all.

During the 1970s and 80s Mr King passed his knowledge down to us, and over the past twenty years we have developed his original technique into a modelled swing that can be taught to anyone, from the wonderfully talented to the woefully inept.

In the time we have been at the School, we have taught tens of thousands of golfers. Sadly, the swings that we see today are no better than those we saw when we first started teaching in the 1970s. How can this be, in an age where golf instruction is such a massive industry?

Golfers of all levels have greater access to more instructional information than

> ## The Golf Delusion:
> The majority of golfers fail to realise that golf must be learnt in the same way that one would learn to speak a foreign language, play a musical instrument or fly an aeroplane. The reason for this is that it is possible for anyone to hit a good golf shot purely by accident.

ever before. Books, magazines, DVDs, online tuition, computer analysis and more bombard the desperate golfer in his search to find the key to this enthralling, if frustrating, game. Yet all this information barely makes a difference. We see the results every day of our working lives and experience has taught us overwhelmingly that almost every golfer naïvely believes that the next golden tip or magic clue will elevate them to a higher level.

Let's face it, it's what everyone hopes for, one quick fix and everything will suddenly fall into place. Unfortunately it's not as easy as that. The majority of golfers fail to realise that golf must be learnt in the same way that one would learn to speak a foreign language, play a musical instrument or fly an aeroplane. The reason for this is that it is possible for anyone to hit a good golf shot purely by accident. Take a bucket of balls, swing the club back and through and even the most un-coordinated would make good contact with a few balls, watching them fly long and straight. This gives the golfer the impression that a few tips here and there will smooth out the rough edges and they will soon be playing good consistent golf, forgetting the fact that maybe only five or six shots from a bucket of balls have been purely struck. Learning a good golf swing is no different to learning anything of value. It must be learnt under controlled

circumstances, slowly, one step at a time and in great detail.

Most golfers don't think this way because of the accidental good shot. For example, you would not be capable of conversing in fluent Cantonese one minute and be unable to utter a single word seconds later; play a musical solo, then moments later not hit a single note; fly the Atlantic, then lack the ability to get the aircraft airborne again. However, this is very much the case in golf. A booming accurate drive can be followed by a huge shank into the woods, a fluff, a top or even an air shot, and often is!

The purpose of this book is to teach you a structured modelled swing; to teach you where to be at each and every stage of your swing and to blend the swing's structure into one beautiful, free-flowing movement. It offers the only guaranteed solution to the 'trial and error' golf played by 90% of golfers. Building swings this way has been our life's work, and if you study this book in great detail we are convinced that it can do the same for you. Every word, every sentence and lesson has been written for a reason, and nothing should be overlooked. It is important to remember that these teachings are not theoretical. They have been proven in well over half a million teaching sessions and will build a sound, solid swing that will last for life.

2

Leslie King 1961

What is the point of curing a slice by planting the germ of a hook which erupts within the next few days? The wretched golfer, overjoyed at losing his slice, is soon in despair again as he struggles on the left hand side of the course instead of the right.

Solving one problem by creating another simply adds to the confusion and depresses his morale. It is negative teaching which can never lead to lasting progress.

My method of instruction is not built upon a vague series of hit and miss experiences, one or other of which may give temporary tidiness to a pupil's game. My aim is a positive one – to build a sound and lasting technique in which all the fundamentals are fitted together into one cohesive swing unit.

I am not prepared to waste time on gimmicks or smart tricks and I will admit at once that I know of no short cuts to success at this fascinating game. It demands hard work and practice before one even begins to master the precise art of delivering the centre of the club face firmly and squarely into the back of the ball and on through into the finish.

There is positively no secret tip which can turn a mediocre player into a good one overnight. Yet there are players struggling vaguely along, pathetically searching for the elixir of a new golfing life in the upper strata of the game.

I have in mind a pupil who came into my school for the first and only time. He really had no swing worth the description. He moved the clubhead sharply back and forwards in a series of wristy jerks.

I set him to work on the first and elementary stage which leads in due course to the shaping of a serviceable swing. I had quickly seen that this player lacked the ability to become good at the game but I could have worked a definite improvement in him had he been prepared to listen to my first instruction.

However, I never saw that pupil again and this is why. Meeting the person who had introduced him to me, he told me that his friend had said that I had treated him as a beginner!

I was genuinely sorry to lose him as a pupil, notwithstanding that I always have more work than I can fit in. My secretary is regularly working on my appointments book for weeks ahead and claims a constant headache as a result. But I could have given him a sound foundation and helped to build a modest but nonetheless rewarding game.

This player, however, quite obviously had a sadly inflated assessment of his own ability and potential. With this attitude of mind he came to me expecting to impress with what he already knew, requiring me to provide the simple tip which would shoot him straightaway into the single-figure handicap class.

He flattered not only himself but me as well. I would work no sudden miracle, I had to treat him as a beginner but he was desperate to run before he could walk.

In sharp contrast is the case of Ian Caldwell, 1961 English Amateur Champion, who came to me at the beginning of 1960 in an unhappy frame of mind about his game.

I decided that his swing needed re-shaping on a major scale and I set to work on him in exactly the same way as I had done with the pupil I have just referred to.

Caldwell, be it noted, was already a good and experienced player with a fine international record behind him. Yet, in a sense, he was more humble than the other man, the raw novice.

He did not expect a golden tip which would solve his problems overnight, and he was not worried when I warned him that what I proposed to do would take some time but would bring about some marked degree of improvement within a few months.

So it proved – four months later he reached the semi-final of the English Amateur Championship.

We kept working on his swing and the following year he won the English Title. Even then I had not completed my task; I was certain that he could get even better

– yet for all his God-given golfing gifts, he had his own complex problems of approach to master, and the measure of his ultimate progress must depend on the extent to which he overcomes these problems.

However, the headway he made under me following a long period of uncertainty was most revealing. He had put his swing into my hands and shown a readiness to work over a period. While the player at the other end of the scale had expected me to produce a gimmick, which would turn him into a golfer overnight, this sort of miracle simply cannot be worked.

Even a noted tournament player like South African Harold Henning was prepared to accept my blunt assessment of his swing. At the suggestion of a friend he came to my school a few years ago and I told him quite frankly that he had a terrible loop in his backswing.

He took my advice and when I next saw him at Royal Birkdale in the 1961 Open Championship, I noted at once that he had smoothed out his backswing and so given himself a very fine clubline into the ball.

Henning remembered how I had advised him and thanked me for what I had told him two or three years earlier when we had last met.

My model offers no trick transition from rabbit to first-class golfer. I gradually shape a sound smooth swing which once acquired will stand up under pressure. Such is my objective with every pupil who comes

D.J., Leslie and Steve in 1984.

to me. I set out to implant in his mind a picture of the shape he needs to acquire, taking him along, stage by stage, until he can sense the shape developing.

Let it be understood that I teach a definite method based on years of experience and proven principles. Various people have their own particular problems arising from characteristics of bone structure and general build. I note these and prescribe accordingly.

But my fundamentals apply in the main to anyone capable of swinging a club through an arc.

The shaping of the swing is all important; once you have it keep it. Don't bend it out of shape by tinkering. This is where many a better-than-average performer leads himself still further off the rails when his game goes temporarily sour on him.
Leslie King 1961

This passage was written by Leslie King nearly fifty years ago. It is as relevant to the amateur golfer today as it was then.

3

Hands of God

Although the general basics of the swing are now well understood by most golfers, the swing's crucial hand line is the least understood and most frequently badly performed movements in the golf swing. It is the main reason why 90% of golfers will never get any better.

In an ideal swing, the hands, arms, body, feet and legs should be moving in a series of chain reactions that shadow each other. No section of the swing should be addressed without considering what goes before or after, nor the section being worked on.

In addition, one part of the body should not be thought about without considering what is happening to the body's other parts. Without question, the swing must always be looked at as a whole.

However, if there is one thing that can be said to be the most important thing in the golf swing, it is the directions that the hands and wrists swing the club, initially through the backswing and subsequently throughout the downswing into the ball and into the follow through. It is this hand and wrist action that most separates the good player from the bad.

The naturally gifted golfer is blessed with hands that control the path of the swing and the clubhead's delivery into the ball and beyond into the finish. It is what he does instinctively. The gifted player's swing shape may vary from the ideal, but he will always maintain control of the clubhead through the essential impact area.

This is why you sometimes see swings that may look a little unorthodox but produce outstanding results and – conversely – you also see swings that may look graceful and flowing yet offer very little. These players may have good fundamentals, but their hands lack the ability to deliver the club squarely, consistently and powerfully into the back of the ball.

The swing of the perennial struggler lacks either of these attributes. They have poor fundamentals and lack any semblance of a clean hand line. These poor souls play year in, year out with the same wretched inconsistency, hoping that the next tip from the top or 'magic cure' will open the gates to a golfing paradise. Sadly, no such cure exists.

The only way an average player can effect a permanent change in their swing is by learning a structured modelled swing that emulates the hand line of the naturally good golfer – those with the God-given talent to deliver the clubhead squarely, powerfully and consistently into the back of the ball.

RIGHT
The naturally gifted golfer is blessed with hands that control the path of the clubhead's delivery into the ball.

4

Some notes on the grip

It is quite rare for the good player to struggle with his grip. Most low handicap golfers have played for years and have established and stabilised their grips very early on.

There are, however, exceptions. One very famous single-figure handicap pupil of ours has an extremely awkward-looking interlocking grip.

If he had the patience and correct mental attitude to change his clumsy ham-fisted grip, great progress to his swing could be made. Unfortunately, he is such a box of tricks that changing his grip would probably cause a complete mental breakdown as he would complicate the process to such a degree that it would not be worth the effort. So, reluctantly, we have to work around his particular grip problem.

The mid-handicapper is fortunate in that he is normally in possession of a serviceable grip that presents no major problems and only slight adjustments are required to bring it up to the School's standard.

The beginner, or struggler, usually possesses a grip that is too weak with the left hand and too strong with the right. In simple terms this means that the left hand is too far to the left of the shaft and the right hand is too far to the right. In both cases this forces the club into the palms of either hand instead of the fingers.

A good way to check your grip is to face on to a mirror with your favourite instruction book or picture of a top-line pro in front of you. Take your grip and address and see how your grip's image compares to that of the ideal.

If you are a beginner or struggler, chances are that you will need to turn your left hand slightly to the right and your right hand slightly to your left. This may indeed feel very strange but this only highlights the fact that in golf the position that you *think* you are in is actually very different to the position you are *actually* in!

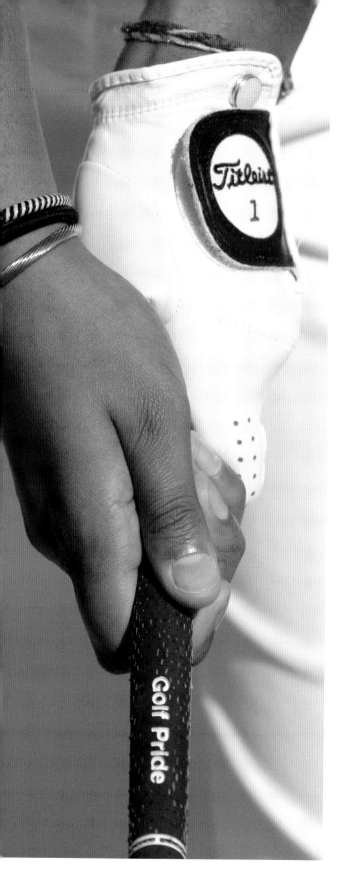

The club should be held in the fingers. As the left hand is placed upon the club it should turn slightly to the right – showing two or three knuckles of the left hand. The right hand should approach the club from the side with the palm facing downwards and close over the thumb.

One aspect of the grip which cannot be seen is the grip's pressure. In our experience we rarely, if ever, see a player who holds the club too lightly but we see plenty who hold it too tightly. Holding the club too tightly makes a correct hand movement very, very difficult to master. The wrists have very little chance of hinging correctly in the backswing and it severely affects the chances of releasing the clubhead into the back of the ball. If you hit the ball straight out to the right and have difficulty performing the backswing hand line correctly, there is a fair chance that you could be gripping the club too tightly.

So how hard should the club be held?

Analogies such as holding the club as if you were 'holding a bird as you take it out of its cage' or 'holding a tube of toothpaste' have much to offer; Leslie King described a feeling of gentle firmness. And we think that this quaint, old-fashioned phase is as good a description as any.

5

The two-handed baseball grip

The interlocking grip

The Vardon overlapping grip

The two-handed baseball grip

The classic Vardon overlapping grip has been taught at the school since the 1950s. It has served thousands of pupils very well and is used by the majority of tour players and leading amateurs.

A number of tour professionals use the interlocking grip where the small finger of the right hand links in between the first and second finger of the left hand. Good strong golfers with God-gifted hands find that by interlocking the fingers they can control any over-zealous hand action. It is the grip used by Tiger Woods, the legendary Jack Nicklaus and our own Juli Inkster, who won two US Opens, was elected to the US Hall of Fame and appears later on in this book.

If you are a good player and have successfully used the interlocking grip,

leave it alone. However, we have found that for the average golfer or perennial struggler the interlocking grip is a definite non-starter. Unlike the talented tour player, the struggler needs as much help as he can in activating and infusing the hands.

The hands must be live and active, controlling the clubhead and swing plane throughout the backswing and downswing; anticipating and making the delivery of the clubhead into the ball. The interlocking grip does very little to help this. In our experience we find that it forces the club into the palms of the hands, thus disconnecting the club from the fingers and destroying the hands' ability to swing freely throughout the swing.

> (Unlike the talented tour player, the struggler needs as much help as he can in activating and infusing the hands)

The origin of the Vardon Grip

Golf clubs of old were very different to those of today and the hickory-shafted clubs of yesteryear were whippy, unreliable and difficult to control.

The two-handed grip was the norm of the day. Good players blessed with good hands often found these shafts too unreliable for consistent golf and, in an effort to cut out the play in the hands and consequently the shaft, they would experiment not only with their swing, but most importantly, their grip.

The overlapping grip was the brainchild of a Scottish amateur, Johnny Laidlay. Harry Vardon (above) adopted this grip as he felt it married his large hands perfectly. From then on the grip became known as the 'overlapping Vardon' grip.

The interlocking grip followed some years later and it is only now, with technology bringing golf clubs under control, that people are returning to the oldest grip in golf, the two-handed baseball grip.

In our experience, average golfers lacking natural talent and power need all ten fingers on the shaft to control the club and swing it through its desired route to deliver the club squarely and powerfully into the impact position and beyond.

We first started using the two-handed grip many years ago in swing drills designed to take out the roll of the wrist on the backswing, in order to deliver the clubhead into the ball with the right hand at impact. After practising with this grip pupils would return to the school having discovered that they actually played better golf if they employed it for all shots. Therefore we strongly suggest that you give the two-handed baseball grip a try.

6

The two-handed grip
A case history

When I first started to play golf I went to the driving range, had a couple of lessons and read a few books just to get me started.

Everything I read and was told recommended that as a lady golfer I should use an interlocking grip. I never really felt comfortable holding the club in that way and my progress, to say the least, was slow. Almost everything I hit went straight out to the right and when I went to the range, I frequently suffered the embarrassment of smashing the ball into the wooden bay divider.

When my husband took me along to the School I was surprised when the first thing I was shown was a ten finger grip. However, as soon as I applied my hands to the club I could feel the difference. Previously the club had felt heavy and

clumsy in my hands, but now I could feel a 'sensitivity' through my fingers. The club felt lighter, controllable.

Having five fingers of the right hand on the club, I could feel how my right hand helped to keep the club on the correct line during the takeaway to halfway back stage.

When it came to actually hitting the ball it was really quite a revelation. For the first time I could feel my hands square the club to the ball at impact and finally understood what was meant by delivery and release. My friends were surprised at how quickly my game had turned around and were also keen to try the two-handed grip. Many of them have now also made a permanent change, achieving similar results and, like myself, cannot recommend it enough!

Susie Hill – Beginner

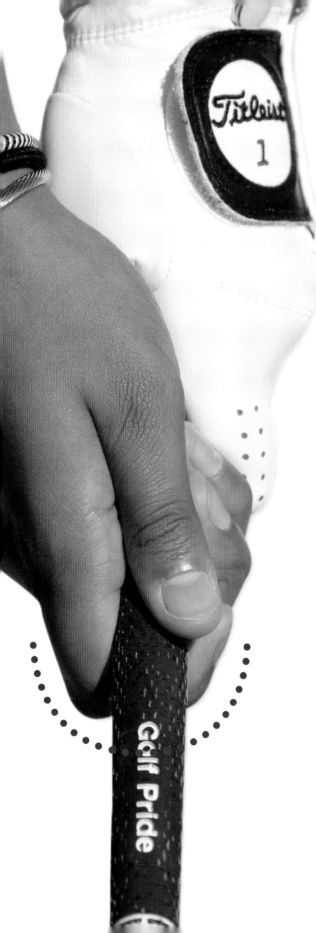

LEFT
The forefinger must be triggered;
pointing away from the other fingers.

7

Whichever grip you choose, you must check this

If you push the ball straight out to the right it means that your hands are blocked or open at impact. This is partly due to inactive lower body movement at impact and is dealt with in detail in later lessons featuring impact and the correctly shaped follow through. This blocked position of the body is nearly always accompanied by inactive hands.

If you have tried the two-handed grip and decided that it's not for you, there is one more thing you must check before you look to your swing for corrections – the placing of the right hand on the club, and especially the forefinger, which must be triggered. Triggered means pointing away from the rest of the fingers. This is vital as it places the finger slightly to the right hand side of the shaft and it is this finger that delivers, along with the right hand, the clubface squarely to the ball.

8

Worse before better?

I t is generally accepted that any major change in a golf swing is going to take time and there's every chance the player may get worse before he gets better.

In the past we would have probably agreed, but over the last ten years our teaching has evolved in such a way that we now believe that getting worse before getting better is a thing of the past – almost all of our students now progress from day one.

The secret lies in learning the swing in what we term 'super slow motion'. Today there is a strong belief that you cannot learn a swing by learning positions and we both agree and disagree with that assessment.

Positions *have* to be learnt. The body, arms, club and hands must swing through the correct positions to keep the club on an arc that will bring the club squarely and powerfully into the back of the ball and beyond into a controlled finish. If the swing

positions are poor (i.e. wrists rolled, static impact, no finish), the club cannot possibly maintain its line. Therefore, unquestionably, positions have to be learnt.

However, where we *do* agree with the 'no position' theorists is that you cannot learn a swing from static positions. Initially, positions must be learnt, but almost immediately the positions must be blended together. Even at the slowest speed the essential sense of momentum

can be felt. The swing will then gradually find its natural speed.

It is this approach to learning and perfecting the swing that has revolutionised our teaching over the last decade and genuinely offers a programme for immediate improvement.

ABOVE
Positions have to be learnt; but almost immediately must be blended together.

9

A lesson at the school

When a pupil first visits the school we are ready for them before they even walk through the door.

As you are by now aware, 9 out of 10 golfers make the same mistakes and we can assure you that this is an absolute fact. Every year, hundreds of new golfers take to the mat and it seems to us that the more books they've read, the more DVDs they've watched and the more lessons they've had, the worse their swings are. In short, they are totally confused! Once we have recorded a new pupil's swing we replay it and take them through it in great detail, explaining how one poor position invariably leads to another in a series of catastrophic chain reactions.

Almost without exception a player will twist or roll the hands and wrists during the takeaway, which immediately destroys the crucial swing plane. From here it is all downhill. At the top of the backswing the club is hopelessly out of position and a good movement through impact and beyond is near impossible.

We then carefully reconstruct the swing, pushing and pulling the pupil through the entire sequence slowly and deliberately, explaining each and every part. In effect the swing is built up frame-by-frame, just as it appears on a slow-motion video replay. This is a concept the pupil can easily understand as they can see what is happening throughout the entire movement. By the end of the first lesson, the student has a complete understanding of where the club should be at each and every stage of the swing and has been given a time-tested programme for immediate improvement.

10

Word of mouth is by far the best form of advertising!

W e don't advertise. There is no exterior sign advertising the school's locality and if you came for a lesson you would swear you had come to the wrong place, as there is not even a reference to the school on the front door. You would be discreetly let in after ringing the Porter's Bell.

Being underground, miles from a golf course and with very little publicity, 90% of our clientele come from word of mouth recommendations. It is a testament to our teaching and must mean that we're doing something right. Even more so when you consider that some pupils won't recommend their friends – because they want to beat them!

This was highlighted when former Chelsea FC star Gianluca Vialli first took lessons. He said he had been trying to see us for ages as he had seen how much his team mate Gianfranco Zola had improved, but Zola wouldn't tell him about us until he had got a lot better than him! Thankfully for us, not all of our clients are so reticent. Hugh Grant is the total opposite. There is probably no other pupil who has recommended the school to more people over the last twenty years.

Husband and wife recommendations are an interesting subject. Either partner has to make the decision whether to recommend the other or not. For them it is a double-edged sword. If they do, they have a golf partner as well as a life partner, they can enjoy their golfing holidays together and they have a shared interest. On the other hand, if they don't they

are free for their regular Sunday morning four ball and golfing weekends with their friends. It's a conundrum that taxes many of our married clients.

Out of every one hundred new pupils, ninety are usually from word-of-mouth recommendations, two or three come from the Yellow Pages, a further two or three from a newspaper or magazine article or the internet. Anyone can log on to www.knightsbridgegolfschool.com and find out about our system, but we still find we have enough enthusiastic students telling the world about us to keep us busy.

On one occasion a resident of our building, on leaving his front door, bumped into a young woman carrying a set of golf clubs.

"Hello," he said. "I recognise you. You're Juli Inkster, US Open Champion. I was watching you on the TV at the weekend and now you are standing in my hallway with a set of golf clubs. This is surreal! What are you doing here?"

"I've come in for my golf lesson," she replied. "In the basement with Steve and Dave. I've just flown six thousand miles from San Francisco for it."

The resident was gobsmacked. He said "I've lived at 47 Lowndes Square for ten years and I've never even realised the school existed. I drive twenty miles for lessons at my club and I'm not getting any better!"

Soon after, the resident became a regular pupil of the school and he now plays off a 7 handicap.

CLOCKWISE FROM BOTTOM-LEFT
D.J. and Steve; the school's unassuming entrance; Hugh Grant one of the School's well-known pupils; Lowndes Square; a pupil in the nets.

The address should anticipate movement

Leslie King was one of the first teachers to emphasis the importance of correct posture at address. He maintained that the top of the back should remain straight and that the body should lean over from the hips with the knees being slightly flexed.

He insisted that a solid, free-flowing swing could only be built from a posture that allowed every consecutive movement in the swing to be carried over from one stage to the next. He was frequently ridiculed for his insistence on correct posture and looking back we can, in all fairness, see the reason why. Professionals who visited the school would enthusiastically return to their clubs and install into their pupils a rather exaggerated version of Mr King's ideal set up. These players would stand rigid with an arched back and far too much bend in their knees. They were locked into a very awkward and uncomfortable position.

This was very clearly illustrated to us one day in the summer of 1978, when Leslie King's teachings were being serialised in a leading golf magazine. The magazine had decided that studio photographs against a stark white background would best illustrate the swing's positions. Studio time, of course, costs money and one day, due to terrible traffic conditions, we were running late for our appointment at the photographer's studio. The magazine's editor, a lovely chap who we still see from time to time, decided that as he had a working knowledge of our system, he would pose the positions himself.

The result, quite frankly, was hilarious. Our editor friend was standing with the top of his back ramrod straight, the small of his back painfully arched and his knees hideously bent. He looked to be in absolute agony! We had to laugh, although we knew that it did nothing whatsoever to further our cause and would hold us up to absolute ridicule. It really now does seem so long ago, but these days teachers are so obsessed with the address that their pupils are fast beginning to look like the uncomfortable editor.

So, what is the true purpose of the address and what is an ideal set up?

The back should be relatively straight, though not stiff. There should be no arch in the small of the back and the knees should be slightly flexed.

Above all, the posture should anticipate movement. It is similar to that of a tennis player waiting on the baseline to receive a serve or a goalkeeper anticipating in which direction the penalty taker will place his shot.

In a nutshell, the address is live and active and anticipates movement.

Positions will vary slightly due to an individual's physical characteristics and the length of club used. Generally, the back should be relatively straight – but not stiff – and the knees should be slightly flexed.

ABOVE LEFT: Christopher Lee, 88, demonstrates perfect body poise at address.

If you approach the ball from behind, the alignment should take care of itself

12

If only I could line up correctly

We have lost count of the number of times a player has told us that they had driven the ball long and straight but it had finished twenty yards to the left or to the right of its intended target.

Then they sigh and say, 'If only I could line up correctly I would be a fine golfer.'

Sadly that analysis is way short of the mark. In most cases the player should look to his swing for corrections, rather than blaming his problems on alignment. Lining up is not exactly advanced mathematics and if you approach the ball from behind, the alignment should almost take care of itself.

If you normally hit the ball straight left of your target your problem is caused by the club swinging slightly across the ball. This could be caused by a lack of shoulder turn on the backswing, which would force the club out of line on the downswing. However, even if the shoulder turn is complete it is still possible for the hands, arms and body to push the club out of line on the downswing.

If your shots finish consistently to the right of the target, chances are that although you may have performed the backswing correctly you are trapped or blocked at impact. A fault suffered by 9 out of 10 golfers reading this book!

13

The inward flexing of the right knee

We recently met a good friend and pupil of ours whom we hadn't seen for some time. After catching up on the latest gossip the conversation naturally turned to his golf swing. He told us that he'd started to point his right knee slightly towards the target at address and was keen to hear our opinion as to whether or not this was good technique. We assured him that it was indeed good technique and something that was once part of our standard swing model. This slight inward flexing of the knee has two main benefits, as our friend had discovered. In the first instance he felt that it stabilised his right knee on the backswing. Secondly, it allowed him to pre-empt the crucial knee, foot and hip movement into impact.

The following day we were reviewing material from Mr King's 1961 instructions book and came across the following passage:

'Whilst warning against exaggeration I must stress that the inward flexing of the right knee is a vitally important feature of the stance.'

So why don't we now recommend it to all and why do we no longer consider it a vitally important feature of the stance?

The answer lies in Mr King's first words. As with a pupil's obsession to keep a straight – almost rigid – back at address, the inward flexing of the knee became grossly exaggerated by the majority of pupils. They would turn the knee in to such an extent that it made a full shoulder and 45 degree hip turn in the backswing impossible, so ultimately it became more of a hindrance than a help.

If, being armed with the dangers of exaggeration, you wish to give it a try, we have no objection. When performed correctly it can be a great help in building good backswing body poise and recreating the live, dynamic impact position of each and every player on tour.

ABOVE The standard right knee position at address
BELOW The inwardly flexed right knee

14

The dangers of the arched back

Thankfully, due to the explosion of interest in golf instruction, the correct posture at address is now well understood and executed by the majority of golfers. However, in pupils' enthusiasm to address the ball with the back straight and eliminate the slovenly posture of golfers past, we are now beginning to see a very different problem.

Increasingly, the hollowed arch of the back is being brought to the school by golfers convinced that the arch in the small of the back is good technique. The hollowed back address is seen in a number of tour professionals, admittedly, but for the average golfer such posture is not recommended and can cause severe discomfort to the lower back. We have adjusted the posture of a number of golfers

The arched, hollowed lower back.

As contorted as this position may look, we frequently see postures as distorted as this.

with instant results. The discomfort they expressed has been eliminated by replacing the arched back with a softer position.

There is a knack to doing this and generally women are far more proficient at feeling this movement than their male counterparts. If you are a male golfer and can't quite get this feeling, you may want to ask your partner's advice! You will be able to tell if you have executed it correctly, as your lower back will feel 'softer' and in a far more comfortable position.

Another reason why an arched back is not good technique is that it restricts the hip, and consequently the shoulder turn, on the backswing. Once again, some tour professionals like to limit their hip movement through the backswing, but the average golfer needs as much help as he can get in turning the body fully.

The 'softer' lower back. Note how the top of the back is still relatively straight.

15

The arched back
A case history

A few months ago I read an article in a golf magazine extolling the virtues of keeping the back straight at address. According to the writer the straight back was a cure for all sorts of problems encountered during the golf swing. It recommended a straight, almost stiff back with the spine arched. The article was lavishly illustrated with lines drawn down the back, through the hips, and covered four or five pages.

Having not paid too much attention to my address posture, I took this advice on board and started to seriously work on my posture and set-up. I wish I hadn't bothered. Within weeks my back was so sore I had to stop playing golf. In all honesty, this was no hardship. The golf I did play was so poor that giving up actually came as something of a relief.

After a few weeks' rest a good friend of mine suggested I visit the Knightsbridge Golf School with a view to starting afresh. I phoned for an appointment and spoke directly with Dave and told him my problems and how they had arisen. Without even seeing me he cured me! He told me how they'd seen so many players suffering due to this obsession with a rigid back set-up and how to go about affecting a cure.

By the time I had my first lesson I was well on the way to recovery. After giving my 'softened' address the once-over, Dave showed me how the arched back had altered the plane of my shoulder and hip turn and how that had contributed to the terrible back pain I had been suffering.

Months later, I have now improved my game significantly and have never had any trouble with my back since making that game-saving phone call.

David Duke – 12 handicap

Tom Weiskopf at the 1971 Masters Tournament.

16

Tom Weiskopf

One of our clients recently showed us a golf magazine, which featured a swing sequence of Tom Weiskopf from 1978. The gist of the article was that the magazine had said thirty-one years ago that it was the definitive golf swing and discussed its relevant parts. Now, thirty-one years later, the magazine concluded that these parts were faulty and that modern teaching shows how these positions could be improved.

We remember, as if it were yesterday, showing Leslie King the original article in 1978 and seeing him exploding with rage and pointing out all the parts that were wrong, (i.e. the hand and arm set at address, the backswing blade angle and the bow back of the body at the finish). All the things that the magazine had concluded were perfect golfing technique. He really was that far ahead of his time!

17

How the video camera has made our work so much easier

Every few weeks we get a call from an old client of ten, twenty, thirty or even forty years ago and are constantly surprised at the swings they bring to the mat. Swings that were built over forty years ago can be compared to the great players of today and are almost identical in their fundamental positions.

A pupil of ours, whom we still see today, took up the game of golf at the age of forty in 1975. He told Leslie King that there was no point in him playing golf if he wasn't going to be any good at it. King told him "If you follow my instructions and do as I tell you, you will have a chance." Mr King didn't let him go on a golf course for six months. Instead, he made him practice in the golf school and in his own back garden. By the time the man was forty-three he was a scratch golfer. This story is typical of others we have heard on numerous occasions over the last thirty years. Mr King built these swings without the aid of any video or computer technology, and against great opposition from a golfing establishment who insisted that you couldn't teach a method in golf and had to work around an individual's mannerisms.

It is fascinating for us to see the amount of golf instruction and teaching systems that have blossomed over the last few years. Even as recently as twenty years ago, 'method' was a dirty word and the idea of an indoor school was looked upon with disdain. Yet these days it seems that an indoor golf school is being opened almost every day, usually equipped with the latest computer technology and simulators.

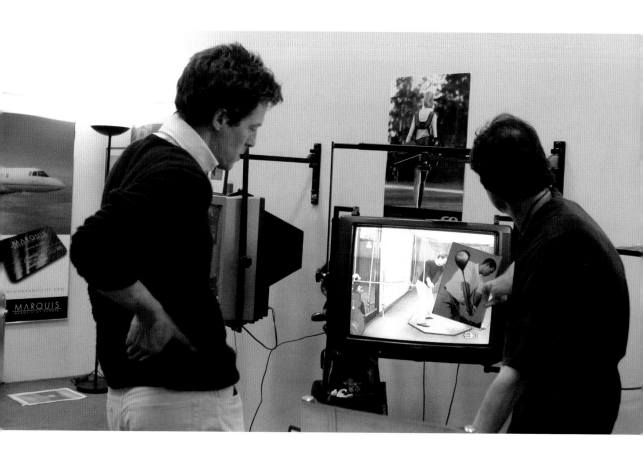

ABOVE/RIGHT
Steve helps Hugh Grant analyse his swing
with the aid of video replay.

The Knightsbridge Golf School was
born in 1951, and for the first thirty years
didn't have any teaching aid other than the
instructor's eyes. In 1985, we started using
video cameras, and their introduction
has proved invaluable. It is not so much
that they help us; it is the students who
benefit, as they can see where they are in
their swing. We, of course, can *already* see
where they are. Years ago, half the lesson
would be spent arguing with pupils about
their positions. They simply wouldn't
believe where they were in their swing.
One of the constant difficulties in the golf
swing is that where you think you are, is
rarely where you *actually* are!

18

Golfer's back

A number of osteopaths and physiotherapists often send their patients to us to learn or improve a swing that best preserves the health of the back.

Golfer's back is caused entirely by bad swing technique and is quite easily addressed by learning how to turn the body through both the backswing and follow through.

Before looking to your swing for corrections, we must first of all take a look at the address and once again warn you of the dangers of an arched lower back. A hollowed lower back is these days mistakenly believed, by some, to be good technique. It is nothing of the sort and can cause serious damage to the lower back. The correct spine angle should be relatively straight but the small of the back should be tucked down and under. The arched back will also inhibit the backswing shoulder turn and render a correct plane of turn an impossibility.

The most common reason for back pain is the tilt or tip of the shoulders on the backswing. This involves dropping the left shoulder down and raising the right shoulder and hip up. This is usually accompanied by a straightening of the right knee. This tilting, tipping movement effectively closes the vertebrae. Turning on a closed vertebrae is a sure way to cause much discomfort to the lower back.

To counter this you must always make sure that your body is turning on a level plane, with the spine angle remaining constant as the shoulders and hips turn over a flexed right knee.

Poor body movement through the finish can also lead to problems with the lower back. Throughout the follow through the spine angle must also remain constant as it does on the backswing. Bending backwards, or a reverse 'C' movement, will invariably put terrible strain on the lower back. So, if you are unfortunate enough to have back problems, we strongly suggest that you look at all the three areas of the swing that could be causing your discomfort.

The swing's crucial DNA

Our programme for immediate improvement outlines the most crucial areas of our swing model – what we term its essential 'DNA'. It addresses the areas where 9 out of 10 golfers make the same mistakes and must be learnt, understood and executed by all standards of golfers.

Takeaway

Learning the correct takeaway hand movement dictates everything that follows, and is the area where 9 out of 10 golfers destroy the swing plane within the first few feet of the takeaway. We call this takeaway to hip height movement 'the master key to good golf' (see page 44) and it is, without question, the most important part of the swing. If you play to a good or average standard, cleaning up the backswing hand line could well provide the breakthrough to a higher level. With good, talented golfers we find that once the hand line has been learnt, everything else just falls into place as their natural talent allows their hands to naturally find their way into impact and beyond.

We have seen proof of this many times, especially when working with tour and club professionals. They find it easy to execute and understand. Often they are amazed that no one has ever taught them, in detail, this most crucial area of the swing. For long-term strugglers an improved hand line offers the only guaranteed solution to sustained long-term improvement. Once the backswing hand line has been learnt you will be in a position to bring the club squarely into the pre-impact position.

Pre-impact

It is vital that the clubface is square by the time it reaches a point six inches before the ball. To do this the club, body and hands must be moving in unison. Pre-impact, the hips must have turned through 45 degrees to allow the club to

TOP LEFT Learning the correct takeaway dictates everything that follows.

TOP MIDDLE It is vital that the clubface is square by the time it reaches a point six inches before the ball.

TOP RIGHT The arms must retain their radius from the centre point of the body through knee to hip height.

swing freely into the swing's apex, the long straight line through the impact area.

Finish

The finish must also be learnt in great detail – it won't just happen. The clubhead must maintain a sustained contact with the ball. The arms must retain their radius from the centre point of the body through knee to hip height.

These three factors are the essential requirements of the swing model – always hold them uppermost in your mind. Each aspect is covered in different parts of this book in more detail.

It is also important to understand that every area of the swing must be learnt in a very specific way. If you simply think

about making a swing change and then proceed to swing the club at your normal speed, you will have very little chance of learning and mastering a new movement. The swing must be learnt in the smallest possible segments, what we term 'super-slow motion'. By moving through the swing one frame at a time, you will be able to feel where the club should be at each and every stage of the swing and correct it if you feel it moving off its intended line.

As the new movements become automatic, the swing will gradually pick up its full speed. The swing should be learnt bit by bit, stage by stage, very slowly, one piece at a time. This must not be overlooked. If you go too fast, any attempt to change your swing for the better will be, quite frankly, impossible.

By twisting or rolling the hands and wrists, 9 out of 10 golfers destroy the swing plane within the first few feet of the takeaway

If you don't think you do, record yourself on video, replay it and think again!

Although most of these players are aware of where they should be at the halfway back stage, they still cannot take the club back correctly and halfway through the backswing, a line drawn through the shaft would be parallel to the ground.

There should be absolutely no roll or twist of the hands and wrists on the backswing. At halfway back the shaft runs between the arms, or to the point of the right arm.

The boxout to the right features first-time visitors to the school and shows how they lose their swings within the first few feet of the takeaway. Although most of these players are aware of where they should be at the halfway stage, they still cannot take the club away correctly. It is vital that you understand that nearly every golfer reading this book is in an almost identical position to the poor souls featured here. The quality of these images is not good – they are not intended to be. These pictures are of real golfers with real swings. They are not posed to show you what not to do, they are the positions that almost every amateur golfer in the world is in at the halfway back stage.

It is critical that you understand this – 90% of golfers reading this book are in this position halfway through the backswing. If you are serious about improving your golf, record yourself on video, replay it and prepare yourself for immediate improvement.

21

9 out of 10 golfers are hopelessly out of position at the top of the backswing

By twisting the hands and wrists in the takeaway, 90% of golfers are out of position at the top of the backswing.

If you don't think you are, record yourself on video, replay it and think again!

A good takeaway to half-way back position makes a good backswing almost certain. From halfway back to the top of the backswing, the shoulders and hips complete the turn as the hands and arms swing the club to the top of the backswing.

22

The most important thing in the golf swing – the 'master key' to good golf

9 out of 10 golfers destroy the swing plane within the first few feet of the takeaway. Learning the correct takeaway to hip height hand line is essential if a golfer wishes to affect a sustained long-term improvement in his standard of play.

The backswing hand line is, without question, the 'master key' to good golf. It is the master key to all the doors in the labyrinth in which so many desperately keen but frustrated players grope and stumble not knowing where to turn. Mastering the hand line and wrist action is the only hope a struggler has of creating a swing plane that replicates that of the naturally gifted player and allows the club to be released squarely, powerfully and consistently into the back of the ball.

We shall shortly be taking you through the backswing hand action in great detail, but before we do we must repeat what was said in previous pages, about learning the backswing in super slow motion. As you take the club back you must try to take

it back as slowly as you possibly can. Not only must you take the club back in super slow motion, you must also stop at each stage illustrated.

By practising the backswing in this manner, you will be able to see and feel at which point the club is moving off line and feel the correction needed to return it to its correct place. By doing this the correction you felt can now be applied the next time you practise it, and this can only be done if you do it in super slow motion. If you try to do it at your normal speed you will have very little chance of making the correction. The club will automatically whip round into the position that it was previously. It's no use thinking that if you don't think about rolling or twisting the wrist, you won't – you will!

Your muscle memory does not know your conscious thought and conscious thought must be applied to change your muscle memory. That's why you have to go through the backswing in this way.

LEFT
The backswing hand line is, without question, the 'master key' to good golf.

As this super slow backswing becomes natural and you are sure you are correctly positioned, the parts can be linked together with the pace of the backswing gradually increasing. You will then be blending one shape into the next with no interruption in the movements.

At this stage we must stress that there is nothing fractured or fragmented about the ideal backswing. We merely teach it in this way to ensure total mastery of each part. Even in slow motion at a quarter of its normal pace a sense of momentum can be felt.

As the swing becomes natural, all your positions transform into a continuous free-following swing. Finally, speed can be blended into the delivery area to produce maximum power.

So learning a great backswing begins with shape, knowing each and every part of the swing. Next comes tempo and rhythm where the shapes are transformed into a natural free-flowing movement.

Backswing hand line sequence

1. The hands and arms initiate the backswing and move the club slightly inside as the left wrist remains at a constant angle.

2. The body now starts to turn over the flexed right knee. The hands and wrists have maintained their position.

5. The hands now hinge slightly upwards. This is the most important stage of the backswing and is where 9 out of 10 golfers destroy their hand line, even if they have performed the takeaway correctly.

6. The hands and arms continue to swing the club upwards. The shaft runs up the line of the right bicep. This is a little steep, but is recommended as an antidote to the rolling, twisting movement suffered by the average golfer.

3. The hands and arms now begin to swing the club upwards as the body continues to turn.

4. Just before hip height the clubhead remains to the right of the hands.

7. The shoulders continue turning as the hands and arms swing the club into the top of the backswing.

8. The backswing hand line is now complete. The hands and arms have swung the club to an angle of 45 degrees, the hands are slightly concave and the face of the club is square.

23

Moulding and shaping a backswing hand line

W e always push and pull our pupils through the swing, moulding and shaping the hand action throughout each stage of the swing. This process not only positions the club correctly but, most importantly, gives the pupil the feeling of a pure hand line, that they can then replicate themselves.

This sequence shows how a pupil is taken through the crucial takeaway to the hip height stage of the backswing. Note how, just before hip height, the clubhead stays to the right-hand side of the hands and arms. This position is slightly exaggerated, as it needs to be to compensate for the endemic wrist roll suffered by the average golfer. From here, we simply move the arm up and hinge the hands and wrists slightly into the perfect halfway back position.

Shaping a backswing hand line

24

Magic move, tragic move

Magic move

Magic move

In the 1970s golf magazines of the day regularly carried an advertisement for an instruction manual that claimed to have discovered the 'magic move' to great golf.

We can't really remember what the magic move was, as we never read it. Even in those days we knew it was just another gimmick or quick-fix solution to the wretched problems suffered by the majority of golfers. We think it had something to do with starting the downswing correctly. That's all very

well, as long as the backswing has been performed in a manner that would allow the mystical magic move to take place.

However, if there is a magic move in golf, it occurs not on the downswing, but far earlier, just before hip height on the backswing. You should already know it as we have already taken you through it during the backswing hand line sequence. Its importance is so great that we have to isolate it and highlight it again here, just to stress how crucial this movement is.

Magic move

Tragic move

Once we have explained and outlined the takeaway, most pupils can take the club back, quite proficiently, to just before hip height. It is the next move, however, that almost all students struggle with. Just before hip height is the point at which the wrists must hinge slightly upwards and you must, while learning, perform this movement at the slowest possible speed.

Unfortunately it is at this stage that 9 out of 10 golfers allow the wrists to roll or twist and drop the club to horizontal – the tragic move!

From seventy years' experience we can say, in the strongest possible terms, that if a 'magic move' exists in golf, this is it. So please read and re-read this page along with the backswing hand line master sequence. It is the most crucial part of our programme for immediate improvement. Once mastered, it will reap dividends for many years to come.

25

Acceptable hand
and shaft angles

The ideal (slightly exaggerated) angle of the hand and shaft line at the hip height stage of the backswing

The more 'classic' hand and shaft angle, where the club runs along the line of the right arm

There should be positively no conscious wrist or forearm rotation in the backswing. The hands and wrists maintain the angle that they were in at the address and simply hinge slightly upwards. The scientific term for this type of movement is 'radial deviation'.

At hip height, ideally, the line of the shaft should run up through the right bicep. It is also acceptable for the shaft to run up the line of the right arm. This is considered a more 'classic' position, though we prefer a slight exaggeration to the angle into the bicep line. The slight exaggeration acts as a safety zone to combat the roll that affects 9 out of 10 golfers. Make no mistake, once the shaft has rolled to beneath the line of the right arm the swing is lost – and with it any chance of consistent shot-making.

26

Flat or upright?

We never talk about a swing as being either flat or upright. A swing may appear upright due to a tip of the body and a high right side, but the arms and hands may have swung the club flat. A swing that, due to a flat shoulder turn, may appear flat could have a hand and arm line that actually makes it upright.

Throughout the backswing and the swing itself, the body and hands and arms must work in unison. The shoulders turn on a relatively flat plane whilst the hands and arms swing upwards to an angle of 45 degrees. The movement is rather like a patting your head whilst rubbing your tummy at the same time.

Naturally, this may take a little getting used to; however it creates the perfect plane as the turn of the shoulders allows the hands and arms to maintain their crucial hand line – the master key to good golf we mentioned previously.

27

Backswing body poise

Most instructional books and DVDs describe the concept of "loading up the backswing to generate power" and "storing energy during the backswing" – the concept being rather like an elastic band: stretch it during the backswing then unleash the "stored energy" during the downswing. A nice theory, but when you consider the biomechanics of the body you come to realise that this is an anatomical and physiological impossibility. Human bodies are not elastic bands and cannot "store energy" during the backswing for subsequent release during the downswing.

Think of a footballer about to take a free kick (a useful analogy to golf, as the ball is stationary). The player positions his body in such a way as to allow a free swing of his leg and foot to the ball. He doesn't pull his leg back against resistance (to store energy); instead he positions his left leg and body to stabilise the position. This then allows him to swing his right leg back and subsequently kick the ball. It is a smooth swing; watch any top player and you can see that they generate enormous power with this method.

The analogies to the golf swing are clear. The golfer uses the body during the golf swing to allow a free swing of the hands and arms. Similarly, the footballer uses his body to allow a free swing of his leg and foot. The end result is the same... a ball moving forwards in the desired direction and with power.

LEFT
The shoulders turn on
a relatively flat plane,
whilst the hands and
arms swing upwards
to 45 degrees.

The hand around the wrist drill

The following exercise will give you the feeling of how the body should turn. In addition, it takes you through impact and into the finish. This is a great exercise as it allows you to make a swing any time you have a few seconds to spare. It was devised by Leslie King in the mid-1950s and has helped thousands to acquire the feeling of a good golf swing. You can practise it standing in front of a mirror; you don't even need enough space to swing a club.

Practise this exercise frequently; it will reap great dividends.

1. Put your right hand around your left wrist and take your address. Now swing your left arm back as you turn your right shoulder and hip into the backswing. Most golfers think of turning the left shoulder, but an easier turn is made from thinking about turning the right shoulder. Throughout the backswing the shoulders must turn on a level plane.

2. At the top of the backswing the left shoulder is on and under the chin. The shoulders should have turned through 90 degrees and the body is centred.

3. From the top of the backswing, swing the hands and arms down to impact with your lower body turning into the ball.

4. As you swing through to the full finish, the right knee and foot has completed its movement, the hips are fully turned and the arms should be opposite the left shoulder.

28

Give it a backhander!

Leslie King was in no way a violent man, but whilst compiling this book we were reminded of an analogy he frequently used when describing the feeling of a correct left shoulder movement on the backswing.

He told his pupils to 'give it a backhander' and, on reflection, we agree that the backhander feeling is highly effective in achieving its objective. You can see this for yourself by performing this very simple exercise. Without a club, lean over, take your address position, put your right arm by your side and let your left hand and arm take its natural address position. The back of the hand should be facing your imagined target and the fingers outstretched. Now simply swing into your backswing as if you were giving someone a backhander!

You will find that the left shoulder maintains its height as it comes around to meet your chin à la Ben Hogan and almost

every pro on tour today. If you try this exercise again, this time placing the right hand around the left wrist, you will again be into the hand around the wrist drill (described on the previous page).

Joe Bugner

Talking of backhanders, we are reminded of an occasion in the early 1970s when Mr King advised the then British Heavyweight Boxing Champion Joe Bugner.

At the time he was teaching legendary boxing commentator Reg Gutteridge and, having watched Bugner's last fight, told Reg that he'd noticed Bugner having trouble in delivering his punches. He appeared frozen, and was having difficulty in freeing his arms and getting them moving.

Mr King was familiar with this problem as he had seen the same sort of thing with many of his pupils who were frozen at address and couldn't get the club moving

Dave demonstrates 'the backhander'.

into the backswing. He told Gutteridge that Bugner's problem was mental. He couldn't move forwards and he would somehow have to redirect his focus to allow him to move forwards again.

Mr King suggested that he should touch his gloves together, as this would free his arms and elbows by pushing them slightly sideways, from where they would again be free to move forwards and allow him to

deliver his blows with maximum force. Mr King was present at Bugner's next fight and noticed that Joe was indeed touching his gloves together and freeing his arms. He recorded a comprehensive points victory.

Now, we know nothing about boxing and are not sure whether this is good technique or not. However, it is a true story and one we had totally forgotten until we advised you to give it a backhander!

29

Telly Savalas

In the early 1980s Hollywood superstar Telly Savalas was a frequent visitor to the school. Like most powerfully built men, he subconsciously believed that his bulk would be an advantage in propelling the ball great distances. This was most certainly not the case and caused him to brace his right leg and to tilt his shoulders as he launched himself into the backswing. He found the hand around the wrist drill to be a great help in changing his backswing body shape and would practise it whenever and wherever he could.

One afternoon we accompanied him on a stroll around Harrods. We were both relatively young at the time and felt quite important walking through perhaps the world's most famous store with one of the world's most famous actors. However, we weren't prepared for what followed.

As we made our way through haberdashery, Telly stopped dead in his tracks, threw his coat to the floor, stood in front of the full-length mirror and performed, to perfection, the hand around the wrist drill! So if, whilst walking through your local DIY store or garden centre, you feel the need to work on your backswing body shape, feel free to do so. You wouldn't be the first.

30

Stuck

It is rare, but on a few occasions we have encountered the problem of a player being stuck at address and being unable to take the club away from the ball.

The problem is mental and over the years has affected many a good player. Sergio García at one time had terrible problems moving his driver into the takeaway.

He gripped and re-gripped the club to such an extent that TV commentators even resorted to counting the number of times he re-gripped. At one stage it reached the extraordinary number of twenty-seven re-grips before he eventually got the swing moving.

We first saw Mr King deal with this problem whilst teaching a former tour player and one time captain of the PGA. His pupil could simply not get the club moving. In this instance, the trick was to redirect his mind by lifting the club two or three inches above the ball, then swing the club slightly forwards past the ball. From here his mind was now free to swing the club into the backswing. Once he had mastered this drill he found it relatively simple to address the ball and take it away in a more conventional manner.

Another way to cure this problem is to take the club back immediately and not to worry about how you hit the ball. The problem is that this is a far more painful process as shot after shot can be wayward in the extreme.

However, once the problem is resolved the player can once again get his swing moving and, consequently, his ball strike back on line.

31

Moving the hands and arms inside keeps the clubhead outside

Maintaining the wrist angle on the backswing is the key to good golf and has to be learnt, performed and committed to memory by golfers of all standards. Even before reading this book, you would probably have been aware of its importance and have tried to maintain a clean backswing hand line, thus eliminating any form of hand or wrist roll.

More often than not, whilst trying to execute the correct hand movement, players inadvertently make their wrist roll worse. The reason for this is that they take their hands and arms straight back from the ball in an effort not to take the clubhead around the body. By doing this the arms become disconnected from the body and the hands and wrists have no alternative but to twist around to the horizontal.

To keep the wrists on line, the takeaway must bring the club slightly inside and the arms and body must maintain their connection and radius from each other, thus allowing the wrists to hinge correctly. Seen from behind, the amateur's left arm must be in line with the left hip at hip height.

Study the pictures of professionals featured throughout this book and you will see that their left arms are a little to the right of the left hip. This is perfectly acceptable for the pro, as from this position they can still maintain their wrists at the correct angle. However, the amateur needs a 'safety zone' and that zone lies in the alignment of the left hip and left arm. By keeping in line, you are much less likely to roll the wrists.

32

Sir Jackie Stewart and the perils of excessive movement

A lot of golf is counter-intuitive. It doesn't seem to make sense. Ben Hogan put it best, perhaps, when he said: "Reverse every natural instinct and do the opposite of what you are inclined to do, and you will probably come very close to having a perfect golf swing."

So when we told Sir Jackie Stewart – Formula One's three-time world champion, one of our students many years ago – that there was too much extraneous movement in his swing, we knew he'd struggle with the idea. After all, everybody does. Surely the golf swing is all about movement?

Stewart, though, began to make real progress when it dawned on him that golf was, in fact, just like driving. It turned out that limiting unnecessary movement had been one of the keys to his racing success.

More pertinently, it had been one of the keys to his survival.

We're not suggesting you play golf as if your life depends on it, of course. It is, after all, supposed to be a game. But if you're still unconvinced about the perils of excessive movement in your swing, and if you still doubt that you're heading for a crash by, say, making a big lateral sway rather than rotating, or by rushing into your downswing rather than accelerating smoothly, well, you could do worse than think of Sir Jackie.

The realisation helped him become a useful golfer, just as it had earlier helped him become a more than useful racing driver. Without it, he might not have become world champion – or, indeed, lived as long as he has.

33

Beware of this advice!

There should be no conscious rotation of the elbows in the backswing. If the takeaway is performed correctly a slight rotation will naturally occur. A conscious desire to rotate the elbows will twist and roll the club into the backswing. This is as certain as night follows day.

Neither should there be any conscious attempt to 'set' the wrist. This advice is becoming ever more popular and brings with it a new problem. Players invariably pick the club up far too steeply and far too quickly. Doing so narrows the arc of the swing and the arms lose their ability to swing freely from the shoulder joints.

The wrist angle should stay constant from the start, hinging slightly and gradually as the arms swing the club freely to the top.

34

Stop at the top

Stopping at the top is a great way to practice. It allows you to complete the backswing with ultimate care and start the downswing on its intended line. This allows you to complete the backswing with absolute precision. Firstly, it removes any impulse to 'hit the ball on the backswing', which causes the body to tilt and the hands to twist or roll on the takeaway. Secondly, it allows you to swing the club down on line and into the back of the ball. Think of an archer as he draws back the bow and pauses momentarily before delivering the arrow to its target.

Whilst learning or rebuilding their swings almost all golfers at the school are taught to stop at the top of the backswing.

Once the swing's old habits have been broken down, stopping at the top will gradually evolve into a very slight pause before evolving again into an imperceptible slow down of the swing as the club changes direction in the transition from backswing to downswing.

There is nothing new or revolutionary about stopping at the top of the backswing. As with all things in golf it has been done for years, and over the decades a host of professionals have used the stop at the top in their practice drills.

When we were teaching on the European tour we met Gordon Brand, a former Ryder Cup player who once finished second in the British Open. Gordon was famous for stopping at the top of the swing, which we admired, as it was something we had done with our pupils for many years. However, we feel that he wasn't happy being seen as something of a novelty on tour and one day called us over to admire his new improved swing, which he confidently told us no longer included a stop at the top.

We watched intently as he rifled shot after shot down the middle of the practice ground, but guess what? – there was still a stop! Which just goes to show that it is difficult to break old habits, but if they're good ones, you don't need to.

RIGHT
The Stop At The Top drill: If you try this drill on the practice ground, you will be surprised how cleanly and far you hit the ball.

The stop at the top drill

1. Tee the ball up.

2. Stop at the top.

3&4. Hit the ball and continue through to a shoulder height finish.

PART TWO
SEEING THE LIGHT

35

J H Taylor

The backswing body shape – pioneered by Leslie King and now used as standard in all golfing textbooks – has its origins in two of the greatest golfers of Leslie King's lifetime.

The flexed right knee was copied from one of the most famous British players ever – J H Taylor. Taylor won five British Opens and enjoyed the most glittering of careers. He retired from tournament golf in 1925 and captained the Ryder Cup Team in 1933. He then settled down to the club professional's job at Royal Mid-Surrey. It was here that Leslie King studied Taylor's swing.

Mr King particularly admired J H Taylor's backswing body poise and how it was based around the flexed right knee which, he felt, created a platform for Taylor's shoulder and hip turn. Convinced of its benefits, Leslie King built the flexed knee into the swings of his pupils with very impressive results. However, J H Taylor told his pupils not to go to "that young fool King" for lessons, as he taught them to keep their right knee flexed on the backswing. As with many great natural players, he didn't realise what he actually did with his own swing, and thought that his knee straightened as he took the club back!

Some years later, with J H Taylor paying more interest in the teaching side of his profession and giving a fair number of lessons himself, an increasing number of Leslie King's Mid-Surrey pupils told him that Taylor was extolling the virtues of the flexed right knee on the backswing. On his next trip to Mid-Surrey, he sought out Taylor, by then a good friend, demanding to know why he was now singing the praises of the flexed right knee, when he had earlier berated Leslie King for doing the same thing. Taylor chuckled, shook Mr King firmly by the hand and said, "There's still a few things that us old fools can learn from you young fools!"

36

Ben Hogan

'The shoulders turn on a level plane'. A universally accepted statement and recognised part of standard golfing technique. However, this wasn't always the case. In golf's early years little thought was given to the pitch of the body on the backswing. However, Leslie King realised that good body poise was essential if his pupils were to get the best use out of their hands and arms.

Years earlier he had built his backswing model around the flexed right knee of J H Taylor. After hours spent watching Ben Hogan, he confirmed his belief that the shoulders should not tilt on the backswing and must maintain their height throughout.

Mr King studied Hogan whenever he got the chance and Hogan's marathon

practice sessions became his marathon study sessions. As Hogan drove hundreds of balls down the practice ground, Mr King noticed how a small patch of perspiration was appearing on Hogan's shirt as his left shoulder came around to meet his chin at the top of the backswing. This confirmed Mr King's belief that the shoulders should turn on a level plane.

Throughout the seventies and early eighties, the backswing body poise was badly abused. Teaching methods such as 'square to square' (which was in fact closed to open) caused players to rock their bodies back and through the swing in order to keep the face of the club square. Players who flirted with this method ended up with a bad back from the pressure directed to the small of the back with the

LEFT
Ben Hogan
RIGHT
Sir Nick Faldo

tilting and turning of the spine. It was not until the mid-1980s that the correct body poise was standardised by David Leadbetter, a former pupil of Leslie King, during his seminal work with Sir Nick Faldo, turning him from shoulder tilter to shoulder turner.

Leadbetter rebuilt Faldo's swing through his body poise. Faldo had already recognised the fragility of his swing and realised that if he were to fulfil his ambitions of being a frequent major winner, he would have to change his swing to achieve greater consistency, to sustain him through the next decade. The result was outstanding and even to this day we use Faldo's 1990s backswing body poise as a perfect example of our ideal backswing model.

37

Sir Michael Bonallack

Many years before Sir Nick Faldo's transformation under David Leadbetter, Leslie King rebuilt the swing of Sir Michael Bonallack in exactly the same way.

Bonallack is generally regarded as Britain's greatest ever amateur golfer. He had already won the amateur championship when he went to Leslie King to reconstruct his swing. Like Faldo, he was aware of his limitations and had an added reason to change: he needed to in order to alleviate the awful back pain he was suffering. This pain was caused by tilting whilst turning the shoulders on the backswing. His problems were so bad that some days he had to retire to bed after playing to keep the pain at a bearable level. The tilting shoulders naturally took their toll on his golf, causing a massive slice which he believes cost him some thirty yards in distance.

Not only did Bonallack's work with Leslie King cure his back problems, it helped him make a clean sweep through all major tournaments on the schedule. He played some spectacular golf including a 61 at Ganton, an unbelievable score. In truth, one aspect of Bonallack's game actually deteriorated whilst working with Leslie King. Before his instruction he had always been regarded as a first-class putter, and needed to be, as he scrambled his way through the scorecard, sinking putts from all over the place to make up for his wild tee shots and greens missed with an iron.

Once he became a player who drove the ball long distances down the middle and peppered the pin with his iron, he stopped feeling the urgency or the pressure with his putter that he previously had and started to drop the odd shot or two on the greens.

Looking back it seems to us that the amateur game was held in higher esteem in those days. Far less media coverage is given to it today than in the past.

Top amateur golfers of the past tended to come from the 'higher ranks' as golf was very much an elitist sport. You had to be reasonably wealthy to devote the time needed to be good and have the right connections to join the clubs that would provide a challenge for the better player. The professional ranks were generally made up by ex-caddies who had lived and breathed the game as they struggled to make a living. The rewards for the successful player were not great and offered no incentive for the comfortably-off amateur to balance his business with a life on tour. It seems

Bonallack (centre, holding trophy) leads Britain to victory against the US in the Walker Cup at St Andrews in 1971.

hard to believe today, with professionals lauded to star status, but years ago the pro was actually looked down on. In fact, up until the 1950s, the poor old pro wasn't even allowed in the clubhouse!

Sir Henry Cotton was one of the first men responsible for changing the image and the status of the professional. Cotton himself was a 'gentleman golfer'. He came from a relatively well-to-do family and when he decided to join the professional ranks caused something of a stir amongst his contemporaries. His professional career was, of course, legendary and he went on to blaze a trail that generations have followed.

The Banning of Sir Henry Cotton

Leslie King and Sir Henry Cotton were good friends, and when Cotton moved to Belgravia he would pop into the School most days to hit a few shots in the spare teaching bay. At the time the School only had room for two golfers. The free bay was constantly in use for practice by regular pupils and was occupied more or less every hour of the day.

Cotton's practising in the school would be the equivalent of us having Tiger Woods joining us every day for a bit of practice. But after this had been going on for a while, Mr King called him into his office and said that he was really sorry but he couldn't allow this arrangement to continue. He explained that his pupils couldn't concentrate on their lessons – they simply wanted to watch Cotton and engage him in conversation; to listen to his stories about his life on tour and his thrilling championship victories. Most importantly, his pupils needed the free bay to practise what they had learnt.

Mr King stressed that it was nothing personal and happily the banning of Sir Henry Cotton from the School made no difference to their relationship – they remained good friends for the rest of their lives.

38

The most important thing in the golf swing
A case history

You would think that after nearly ten years of playing golf and playing off a +1 handicap, I would know how to perform the relatively simple task of taking the club back. Well, I can honestly say that it hasn't been so easy; in fact, it's been an epic journey – one which has taken me all over the world and had me spend what has felt like an eternity listening to teaching professionals giving me their opinion on what I should be doing. I've hit balls off my knees; with towels under my arm; stood on one leg; hit shots one-handed; all of which would be great if I was doing a trick shot clinic, but less great when all you want to do is learn how to take the club back. After years of hearing drivel from numerous professionals, I was left with no choice but to give up golf, as I was so confused and disheartened I could no longer get enjoyment from the game I once loved so much.

However, about a year ago, just as I was about to sell my clubs and join the golfing scrapheap, I was recommended to try the Knightsbridge Golf School. I thought, "Maybe these guys actually know what they're talking about!" So I booked a lesson with Dave and took the long walk down the stairs to the basement, where I felt like I was going to see some kind of doctor for this incurable golfing disease I seemed to have contracted. We chatted and then came the moment of truth: we recorded some of my swings! It became quite evident that I was struggling with the first two feet of the swing. But there and then, on the first lesson, to my amazement, I was being told how to swing the club back.

So, here I am: a totally different golfer; one who is setting off on a new adventure not to simply find the golf swing, but instead trying to perfect it. It is safe to say that whatever I achieve in this game is a direct result of the knowledge that Dave and Steve have shared with me over the past year. I will forever be indebted to them as they walked me through what felt like the longest two feet of my life.

Gareth Gillatt (+1 Handicap)

39

Juli Inkster

When Leslie King's self-published instruction manual was released in the mid-seventies it slowly made its way across the Atlantic. It wasn't published by a major publishing house and relied solely on word-of-mouth recommendation. But soon after it resulted in a small group of pupils making the trip to Knightsbridge from the West Coast of America.

One young golf pro was given the book by a small community of Leslie King disciples residing in the leafy Los Altos area of San Francisco. Brian Inkster was a fine young professional searching for a sound method to further his playing career and a reliable teaching system to fall back on if he failed to make it on the US Tour. Having devoured King's book, he decided to make the pilgrimage to London and spent a month working under the hands of the old master and his teaching assistants. Like many Americans, his enthusiasm and appetite for hard work paid great dividends and every year he would make the trip to learn every possible thing he could. One year he excitedly presented to Leslie King a contact strip of photographs he had of an up-and-coming young protégé with phenomenal talent and a rather unorthodox golf swing. Brian was intrigued to hear what Leslie King had to say about his charge and couldn't wait to see what he would recommend.

Mr King took one look, shook his head and said he was best to leave it alone. Juli Simpson was already a very low single handicap player and the changes required would probably be too difficult and take too long to make. Brian responded by saying that Mr King had previously told him that with a method any changes could be made, over time, to any swing. He convinced Mr King that he was up to the job of re-shaping Juli's swing. Mr King admired Brian's determination, so went through Juli's swing bit by bit outlining every move needed to take his pupil to a different level.

After returning to the US, Brian would regularly call the school with news of Juli's progress and ask for advice on dealing with any problems that came up. On one occasion, he added that they were now a couple and about to become engaged! As a young married couple they spent all their early vacations in London, working on Juli's swing. Their hard work paid off. Juli won three US Amateur titles in succession before turning pro and claiming two US Opens, along with a raft of tour victories.

Juli continued flying over for lessons with us long after Leslie King's retirement, and one year we spent many weeks in Los Altos on an exchange visit. We exchanged our London clientele for a Californian clientele and spent many weeks working in the sunshine with our student's peers. A great time was had by all. Needless to say, California was a golfer's wonderland,

ABOVE A newspaper clipping of Juli Inkster with Steve and Dave.

LEFT Juli, Women's British Open, 2008.

blessed with great weather and the latest golfing know-how. Also, needless to say, 90% of Californian golfers shared exactly the same faults as 90% of London golfers!

We were reunited with Brian and Juli at the 2008 Women's British Open. We hadn't seen them for over ten years, but after eighteen holes and half an hour on the practice ground it felt like they had never been away. The following day, Juli shot 65, seven under par and led the British Open. Brian and Juli had not changed, they were both as charming and natural as ever. What had changed was the Ladies Tour and the standard of those playing it.

In the 1970s we accompanied Mr King to a tournament at Fulford Heath Golf Club, near Birmingham, to assist him in teaching his professional pupils. The standard was, quite frankly, poor. We saw shanked shots, topped shots, air shots and worse, and were witness to Mr King shaking his head and lamenting that the Ladies Tour would never catch on. Well, we are pleased to say that was probably the only occasion he was ever proved wrong! The standard of swings is now very, very good. The players all work through their swings systematically, just as a pupil of ours would, and the purity of their ball striking is certainly a match for the men.

40

The wrists are still rolling

We recently read an article by Italian footballing legend Gianluca Vialli, an ex-pupil of ours. Luca was talking about his love for the game and how, despite spending a lot of money on lessons, he wasn't really as good at golf as he thought he should be. It was quite sad for us to read this because under our hands Luca was well on his way to becoming a low single handicap golfer. He took about a dozen lessons in the spring of 2000 and we accompanied him during a few practice rounds at Stoke Park. He was great company, a lovely man and potentially a very fine golfer. His particular swing fault was, of course, the twist and roll of the hands and wrists during the takeaway. The same fault suffered by 9 out of 10 golfers.

We had almost eradicated this evil movement. A few more sessions would have ingrained the new hand line into his system and his hands would have been free to deliver the clubhead consistently into the back of the ball and beyond. Once he had held this hand line for a few months he'd have never looked back; it would have grown stronger and stronger. Unfortunately we never got the chance. Quite suddenly, he was dismissed as Chelsea manager and we didn't see him again until five years later at a golf day organised by another pupil of ours, Radio One's DJ Spoony.

We watched him hit a few shots and, sure enough, the clubhead once again slipped around his body as his hands and wrists rolled the club into the takeaway.

We couldn't make any alteration to his swing; he was due on the tee within five minutes, so making a change would have been madness.

When he had completed his round we had a chat with him and he told us that he was convinced that he had cured his rolling wrists a long time ago and

LEFT
Gianluca Vialli

must have developed a new problem. Unfortunately Luca's assessment of his swing was wildly inaccurate, but it was what we expected to hear. It is very, very rare for a golfer to suddenly develop a new fault. It is possible, especially if a new movement has caused a reaction in another area of the swing, but generally, and quite categorically, it is the old problem rearing its ugly head.

It is imperative that all golfers eradicate every elementary trace of the roll out of the backswing by learning and maintaining golf's master key.

The roll is like a weed. If it is not removed completely, any hint that is left in the takeaway will invariably work its way back into the swing and down through the pitching and chipping action.

We haven't seen Luca for some time. Hopefully he's found a cure to his problem from somewhere, but if not, of course our doors are always open...

41

This is not a wrist roll

As you read this book and learn about the dangers of rolling wrists, you may be surprised to see, the next time you are watching a tournament on TV, that a number of tour players appear to be twisting the club into the backswing – the very thing we have warned you about throughout. We'd agree that this is exactly what these great players appear to be doing, but actually they are not. Their movement is quite different and is, in fact, a backward break of the right hand.

Such a movement is highly effective and, if performed correctly with its compensatory movement in the downswing, can produce outstanding results. However, this movement cannot be taught to the average golfer, as it distorts the arc of the backswing, causing many complications.

The easiest backswing route is the simplest backswing route. This is achieved by keeping the hands and wrists constant throughout the entire backswing.

LEFT
Don't confuse the backward break of the right hand with a wrist roll. Ross Fisher incorporates this into his takeaway. Nonetheless, he possesses a great golf swing and is a superb striker of the golf ball.

42

The Last Chance Saloon

A few years ago I found myself, for want of anything better to do, absent-mindedly flicking through an article about the Knightsbridge Golf School whilst dozing on the London to Brighton train. I was vaguely interested in the subject, I suppose – even if, horribly frustrated by my ineptitude, I had given up playing golf a few years previously. The low point had come when I had lost a match against my thirteen-year-old nephew. Losing to my three brothers had become an annual event, but losing to a chicken-drumstick of a nephew seemed somewhat beyond the pale.

And then, somewhere between East Croydon and Gatwick, I read a paragraph about the dangers of rolling your wrists. I sat up with a start – I had always thought you were meant to roll your wrists! Rolling wrists had been one of my trademarks…

It is not an exaggeration to say that those words changed my life. Within a few weeks I had arrived at 47 Lowndes Square for my first lesson, within a month I had joined my first golf club, and within a year my handicap had fallen from a generous 24 to 10.2. I even ended up writing a book on my experiences.

I still drop in to see Steve Gould and Dave Wilkinson whenever I get to London. The school has a very special place in my heart. Steve, Dave and Andy Pharro (their right-hand man), who were presented with the dubious pleasure of trying to make sense of my forty-nine-year-old 'swing' – if, indeed, I ever possessed anything coherent enough to be called a swing – gave golf and its pleasures back to me.

I am not saying they know the secret of the golf swing. There is clearly no such thing. But I truly believe that their method, inherited from Leslie King, represents the simplest, most logical and thus easiest route to mastering the art.

So what did I learn, I am often asked? How did I manage to improve by fourteen shots in those twelve months?

I always offer the same advice in reply.

1. The wrists must not roll, either in takeaway or through impact.
2. Concentrate on a connected body turn rather than an independent hit with the arms and hands.
3. Go and ask the guys at the Knightsbridge Golf School – they'll be able to explain it an awful lot better than I can.

Of course, there was a bit more to it than that. It took me a whole book, in fact, to collect my thoughts on the subject. But the advice listed above is as good a starting point as I can imagine. I also learnt that

Andy Pharro takes one of the School's students through his swing

you have to work at it. We live in a three-minute-fix society, where impatience is king. Golf, though, will never be a three-minute-fix of a game. I think that Andy, better than anyone, taught me that.

I asked him from our first meeting to be honest with me, and so he was – brutally so, in fact. He told me, in agricultural Anglo-Saxon, just how bad my swing was. And believe me, it was shocking – more Fatty Arbuckle than Ernie Els. And then he spent the next three months giving me the same lesson, over and over again. We worked on my takeaway, and we worked and we worked. There was no point, he said, in taking the club further back than eight o'clock if my hand line wasn't right. All I'd succeed in doing would be to infect the rest of my swing with errors and unnecessary complications.

I found it very frustrating but Andy, of course, was right. No pain, no gain. I'm not sure many teachers would have dared be as honest with their students. In a world dedicated to instant satisfaction, his approach almost smacked of professional suicide. But we stuck with it and it worked.

He and the School were my last chance saloon. Since then, I've beaten all three of my brothers and I've even managed success against my nephew (who is now a 6ft 3ins rugby-playing monster). I've managed one round of golf of 4 over par, and a couple of 300-yard drives. Most importantly, though, I now play golf rather than assault the game. There can be few greater pleasures.

By Tony Lawrence, author of *Hacked Off, One Man's All-or-nothing Bid to Crack the Secret of Golf (Aurum)*

43

Woods and Irons – a comparison

Woods

The swing with both woods and irons is the same. They look slightly different, but that is down to the length of the shaft. With the shorter-shafted iron, the body is naturally at a lower angle and the shaft of the club at the completion of the backswing is short of the horizontal.

The angle of the body is not so pronounced with the wood, as the shaft's greater length ensures that it reaches a stage that is horizontal to the ground at the top of the backswing.

The iron's angle into the ball is steeper, delivering a descending blow, in contrast to the more sweeping action of the wood. Once again this is down to the variance in length of the shaft and no attempt should be made to play woods and irons differently.

$\left(\begin{array}{c}\text{No attempt should be made to}\\\text{play woods and irons differently}\end{array}\right)$

Irons

A minority prefer to use their woods, but for most they present more of a challenge. Even the tour player will suffer more with a driver than with any other club. This is due to the wood's additional length naturally creating a rounder arc at impact, as opposed to the iron where a straighter apex at impact is more easily achieved. Also, the wood's straighter face imparts more sidespin when mishit than the more lofted iron that diminishes the effect of a round impact line.

Fortunately, technology has made the playing of wooden clubs today far easier than it was for previous generations of golfers. This improvement means that more golfers get the chance to enjoy the feel of a long, straight drive, whatever standard they play at.

44

9 out of 10 golfers are static at impact

*If you don't think you are, record yourself
on video, replay it and think again!*

The body and hips are blocked, the arms are trapped and the hands have no chance of maintaining control of the clubhead through the finish.

Yet 90% of tour professionals are in a dynamic position (shown left) at impact. They hit the ball with the whole right-hand side of the body clearing to allow the hands and clubhead to travel cleanly through the ball.

The static lower body position is common to 90% of amateurs. It is a frightening thought that with the help of years and years of golf magazines, DVDs, books, training aids, golf channels etc., visitors to the school are nowhere near where they need to be at the business end of the golf swing – the impact position. The very thing that drives the ball forwards!

45

How to start the downswing

As your hands and arms swing the club down, the hips and body must respond immediately and move in unison with the arms to correctly position the club at the halfway down stage.

When we first started teaching in the 1970s the majority of golfers initiated the downswing by turning the shoulders and hips, resulting in the body turning over dead legs and culminating in a monumental slice. This can, in part, be attributed to the favoured teaching of the day, which encouraged players to turn the hips (or initiate the downswing) from the top of the backswing. This, in turn, can generally be traced back to a misinterpretation of Ben Hogan's *Modern Fundamentals of Golf*, one of the most famous golfing manuals of

all time. Hogan stated that players must turn their hips from the top of the backswing. Unfortunately, to turn the hips without turning the shoulders is almost impossible and is the origin of error.

In 1974, Leslie King wrote that the downswing should begin with a downward swing of the hands and arms. Visitors to the school showed that this advice in itself had bought with it the opposite problem. Pupils would now, and still do, swing the arms only, resulting in a completely blocked impact position, culminating in a monumental push.

These faults highlight a major problem in seeing one part of the swing in isolation without considering what goes either before, or after, the area of the swing under review. If pupils had studied the instruction as a whole, they would have realised that Leslie King said that the hands and arms initiate the downswing and that the body responds immediately with a slight lateral shift of the hips. Which brings us back to the first paragraph at the top of the page:

As your hands and arms swing the club down, the hip and body must respond immediately and move in unison with the arms to correctly position the club at the halfway down stage.

If you take a look at the pictures opposite you'll probably think that these tour players have pulled the club down stiff-wristed into the pre-release position. Nothing could be further from the truth! The hand and wrist action should be fluid, supple and about as far removed from stiff-wristed as possible. There should be no flail of the wrists, but a very distinctive play in the wrists, with the wrists live and active as the arms swing down.

This is impossible to see in still photography, even though they have swung the club down in the manner described. There is no getting away from the fact that in these pictures they look as if they have chopped the club down. We can assure you they have not.

If the average player tries to pull the club down to replicate what he believes the pros have felt as they reached this position, he will hit the ball with a monumental push.

The correct downswing is felt from a fluidity of the hands and wrists. The hands, wrists and arms swing the club down to halfway. From there, the right hand takes over and delivers the clubhead to the ball. The right hand moves in unison with the body and continues to control the club through the quarter and half finish.

Overleaf is a great exercise to help you get the feeling of how to initiate the downswing and prepare you for the crucial impact.

How to start the downswing and learn a delivery *A case history*

Whilst writing this lesson our thoughts went back to the late 1970s when one good old client of ours had terrible trouble turning his shoulders from the top of the backswing, bringing the club over and across the ball. He put this down to reading Ben Hogan's *Modern Fundamentals of Golf* and trying to start his downswing with a turn of the hips. As discussed earlier, it is virtually impossible to turn the hips without turning the shoulders and the poor chap spent many months slicing his way around the golf course. Once we had improved his follow through and shaped his backswing, we taught him the exercise overleaf and he loved it. In fact he made it his own and it stayed with him permanently!

He found it so helpful and he hit the ball so much better that he actually played around the golf course, stopping at the top, pumping his arms up and down and thumping it!

Did it affect his handicap? Well he certainly looked strange; he was the talk of the club and the butt of many a joke, but as for his handicap, yes, it changed from 15 to 7.

Pump the arms exercise

1. Take the address.

2. Swing the club back to the top of the backswing.

3–6. Now simply swing your arms freely up and down, ensuring that your lower body is moving in tandem.

7–8. Hit the ball and continue on to a full finish.

46

The reflex is the enemy of all golfers

In the vast majority of ball games a fast reflex is essential. It is the prerequisite of the good footballer, tennis player, cricketer and almost every other sportsman who competes in their chosen game.

Their reflex allows them to get to the ball before it gets past them or, in a team game, goes to a member of the opposite side. However, in golf, it is quite different. The reflex is the enemy of all golfers. Any involuntary reflex movement of the hands, arms or body pushes the club off its intended line.

Even at the highest level, the involuntary reflex is responsible for ruining the scorecard of many a potential tournament-winning golfer. Think back to the occasions when you have seen a tournament leader pop his tee shot into the trees, the water or onto an alien fairway. Their natural tempo has deserted them as their reflex has reared up and pushed the club away from its intended line.

The reflex is also responsible for the subconscious effort of trying to steer the ball safely down the middle, despite the player's conscious desire to simply repeat his everyday swing.

Leslie King often told his better players to place their tongue between their teeth. Next time you go to the practice ground, give it a try. It could provide a painful reminder of just how dangerous the involuntary reflex can be!

47

The delivery

Once the foundations have been laid, the structure of the swing is secure; the arc of the swing is constant and the apex repeats and repeats with precision, then – and only then – can your raw talent and strength be discovered.

The delivery is the concentration of pressure, speed and power at the point of impact. The force should always be in the direction of the target, never away from it. As Ben Hogan once said, most people do the exact opposite.

The conscious mind, intimidated by imagining the force required to move the ball vast distances, is sabotaged by the reflex and produces power too early, most usually during the backswing, with the speed travelling in the wrong direction – away from the ball.

Most often the easiest way to subdue the reflex and bypass the conscious mind is through natural imitation, by copying the very good player. Once conscious thought is eliminated you will find a rhythm that fits the beat of your heart and the speed of your mind, an innate ability that shifts the whole process from the conscious mind with its meddling imperfections to the natural coordination of the subconscious, and then onwards to the point at which you play by feel and instinct.

LEFT
Delivery – concentration of pressure, speed and power at the point of impact.

48

Making a delivery

The game of golf is very much a battle between the conscious and the subconscious mind. You can think of making a position. You can think of making a shape to the swing. But the blending of a delivery into the shape must be done by training the hands and the clubhead to react subconsciously. That is, by imitating the intention which is portrayed in your practice swing.

If a player is so absorbed in the delivery that he is over-eager to make it, his reflexes take over from the top of the backswing. His intention races too far ahead and the action is doomed to be rushed and distorted. Hence the time-worn phrase 'hitting from the top'.

Many who remain poor players, despairing of making any progress, keep themselves in the toils for two main reasons. Firstly, they fail to complete the backswing and learn the correct hand line essential to good golf. Secondly, they are far too anxious to get the club back to the ball in the return movement, and are woefully out of position at impact.

You must train yourself to make a delivery to the ball within the framework of a shaped swing by subconsciously sensing the action involved. With many players the swing has blacked out from the time they have taken the club back a few feet from the ball until the stroke has been played for better or worse – usually worse.

It is one thing to acquire a shaped swing which leads you to a poised position at the top of the backswing and through into the follow through. But this in itself is not sufficient. The striking of the ball demands more than setting to one end at the top of the backswing and another end at the follow through in the vague belief that something will happen in the middle.

This is another reason why learning to play golf well with a method which will prove lasting is a slow, gradual process. Many a young player with a good-looking swing, outwardly full of promise, eventually arrives at a stage where his game fails to develop further. Often this is because he has failed to learn to make a delivery of the clubhead consistently to the ball.

We have explained that the modelled golf swing is a coordinated series of actions enabling the player to take up a number of poised and balanced positions with the object of generating and retaining the power and feel in the hands. The hands

Making a delivery exercise

1. Tee the ball up and take the address.

2. Swing the club back to the top of the backswing.

3&4. Swing the club down and stop six inches before impact. The face of the club should be square and the ball should be in the middle of the clubface.

are like an electric battery: they must be charged and kept charged by the actions of other parts of the mechanism.

These actions are blended into a smooth rhythm overall movement by good timing. If the timing from one position to the next is rushed as, for example, in the case of the player who cannot wait to get back to the ball from the top of the swing, the power and feel depart from the hands and an effective delivery to the ball is impaired, almost beyond salvation.

This is why those struggling golfers whose swing has blacked out after the initial stage of the backswing hit many more bad shots than good. Their successful shots are more or less accidental and cannot be repeated with any degree of certainty. We cannot stress too strongly the need to give yourself time and room in which to swing the clubhead and deliver it squarely into the back of the ball. The good, experienced golfer senses the downswing even as he approaches the top of the backswing.

In order to effect a smooth transition from the backswing into the downswing, the hand action, though never hurried, must be even slower in the final stages of the backswing. The hands and clubhead are going to be put into reverse and the operation must be done as smoothly as a skilled driver reverses his car. This feeling helps to give you that almost imperceptible pause at the top of the backswing as the hands begin to change direction.

The downswing should start with a slow downward swing of the hands and arms. Simultaneously, the weight should shift down onto the left foot, the furthest point from the hands. At hip height the hips should be back to where they were at address. When performed correctly this movement gives the hands room in which to deliver the club into the back of the ball.

The art of making a delivery within the framework of a shaped swing will not be learnt overnight. However, mastery of the following exercise will reap instant reward and give you a total understanding of how the blade of the club must be square at a point six inches before impact. The object of the exercise is to increase hand control of the clubhead as it reaches the impact position. Most strugglers will find that as they bring the club into the pre-impact position, they have the face of the club open and they will need to release the club a little more with the right hand. Good players tend to suffer from the opposite problem. Their active hand tends to push or turn the blade over. In this instance the player will need to feel a little firmer in the left hand.

Remember that whilst you are aiming to stop at pre-impact, the club must still be swung down. Work on this exercise and train yourself and your hands to master it. Pre-squaring the blade six inches before impact is the second part of the swing's DNA.

The first, of course, is the backswing hand line, and we must stress, again, that if your backswing hand line is faulty you will have very little chance of squaring the clubface as it approaches the impact position, so at this stage, before moving on, we suggest that you once again check your backswing hand line, the master key to good golf. Without it you will have very little chance of progressing.

Golf tips are like aspirin. One may do you good but if you swallow the whole bottle you will be lucky to survive
Harvey Penick

49

Power source

It is difficult to be perpetually out-driven, especially if you are bigger and burlier than your golfing partners. The temptation is to hit the ball with all your might to show them that you are just as strong as they are. You grit your teeth, brace yourself and wham! Unfortunately, instead of finishing furthest down the fairway you will probably find that you've skied it half the distance or are in awful trouble on either side of the fairway.

Heaven knows it is difficult enough to control the subconscious reflex, but consciously trying to hit the ball into next week is sheer madness.

Power comes from a swing that is technically sound and possesses the pure hand line of the naturally gifted golfer. An action that swings smoothly through its component parts delivers maximum velocity through the impact area and beyond. Even the slightest desire to hit at the ball may destroy the swing plane – and the scorecard with it.

To give you an idea of tempo and a feeling of the swing's motion, we'd like you to consider an unusual, but highly effective, analogy. If you were to drive a stake into the ground, you would swing the hammer head smoothly and unhurriedly up on your hands and arms and almost drop it onto the stake. The deeper you wished to plant the stake the slower you would swing your arms. Essentially the speed would be going the right way, not up into your upswing, but down onto your target.

Similarly, if you were to hammer a nail into a piece of wood, the deeper you wished to drive the nail, the smoother your swing would be. If you wanted to drive the nail only a short way into the wood, you would use short, sharp, fast strokes.

Now contrast this with the golfer who, in desperation for extra length, snatches the club away from the ball and throws it forward on the way down. The speed of the swing is in the wrong places, in the takeaway and at the start of the downswing. The club is actually decelerating as it approaches the ball and the speed is going the wrong way.

The face of the club must be square six inches before impact.

50

Pre square the blade

The face of the club must be square six inches before impact. Every tour player in the world achieves this ideal and it is essential to driving the ball accurately and powerfully forwards.

When teaching the downswing and delivery, we place a coin six inches in front of the ball. The pupil is then taught to swing the club down and stop at the point of the coin. This exercise has to be done at a fairly slow speed, but mastering this drill is a prerequisite of a sound, consistent delivery into the golf ball.

Try this drill yourself, but ensure that your body is moving in a way that allows the squaring of the blade to take place. The image above is a superb example of the tour player's position prior to impact. It should be replicated by golfers of all standards if a sustained, long-term improvement is to take place.

The carpet beater

The impact bag is a fairly recent idea. However, many years ago, Leslie King used to liken the delivery movement to that of the carpet beater, and used to encourage his pupils to hang their living-room rugs from the old Siegfried washing line that adorned almost every garden around the middle of the last century. He then told them to address the rug, make a full backswing and swing the club into the rug, making sure that the blade was square and that the lower body was moving into the impact.

51

The impact bag

Once you have mastered the pre-impact exercise you are ready to move onto the impact bag drill. The impact bag is available from pro shops or online and comes flat-packed. Simply fill it with towels or old clothes and you are ready to go. If you can't get hold of one, a flat-sided holdall or something similar will suffice.

The drill is exactly the same at the pre-square exercise. The only difference is that this time you must move beyond pre-impact into the impact bag. To begin with you must do it slowly and then gradually increase the speed. Its purpose, of course, is to bring the blade squarely into the impact bag. Once again, most poor players will find that they have difficulty in squaring the blade and will approach impact with the face open, as if they were playing a cover drive in cricket. This open position will also be accompanied by a static lower body, a fault suffered by 9 out of 10 golfers.

LEFT Anton DuBeke on the impact bag.

IMPACT BAG™

"The Moment of Truth"

52

Sir Sean Connery and Ian Caldwell

Sir Sean Connery is one of the most instantly recognisable stars on the planet: eternally famous for his signature role as James Bond and one of the first people you think of when the term 'celebrity golfer' is mentioned. In short, he loves his golf. However, it may come as a surprise to learn that he had little interest in the game before his epic clash with the infamous Goldfinger – probably the most famous match in the history of golf. US golfers are well aware of the legendary battles in golf's folklore: Vardon vs Taylor, Hogan vs Snead and Nicklaus vs Watson.

If quizzed, however, much of the general public would probably think of Bond vs Goldfinger: a contest seen by tens of millions of people.

Shortly before filming *Goldfinger* he told his dentist, Ian Caldwell, who was at the time English Amateur Champion, that he had to learn to play golf for the latest film in the James Bond series. Ian had recently secured his first National Title by winning the English Amateur Championship after working on his swing

with Leslie King. He had tried other teachers without success and they had never given him the necessary technical push to win an amateur 'major'. He told Sean that the only man who could make him look a convincing golfer was the man who had finally helped Ian achieve his own personal ambition.

Ian popped into the School recently with his son, now also a regular, and a fine +2 golfer. He told us of his Amateur Championship and his recollection of the final holes of a nerve-jangling afternoon.

Coming up the 15th hole, Ian had a four-hole lead and was dormy four. All he had to do was keep his nerve and the English Amateur Championship was his. Unfortunately, keeping his nerve was not easy. He lost the 15th, lost the 16th and then he lost the 17th. He couldn't hit one decent shot. He slashed at his drive, tried to manipulate his approach shots and yipped his putts.

He needed at least a half at the 18th to win. After a nervous drive and half hit iron, he faced an 80-yard pitch, which

he had to hit stone dead if he was to fulfil his dreams. As he approached the ball, he asked himself what he could do and replied, "I'm now going to be in the Golf School. I am standing on the mat and Mr King is teaching me, telling me just to concentrate on the swing and not to worry about the ball, just make a movement through it and not try and hit it." He made the most excellent of swings and the ball finished six inches from the cup. The title was his.

Forty years later, we still can't think of a better mental approach when faced with any golf shot, especially a high-pressure shot. Think of Frenchman Jean Van der Velde at the 1999 Open. If his mental approach had been the same as Ian's, he would have gone

down in history as a winner of the most prestigious title in golf.

Sir Sean Connery continued seeing Leslie King long after the completion of *Goldfinger*. He became an avid golfer and, in later years, bought his wife and son in for lessons. We haven't seen Sean for over thirty years. However, a short while ago a young woman resident of Barbados came in for a series of lessons. As is the norm we asked her who recommended her and she told us it was Sean Connery.

Coincidentally, *Goldfinger* was filmed at Stoke Park, a lovely parkland course in Buckinghamshire which has been our sister club for the past fifteen years. It is where we take our students to fine-tune their swings and the first place we take our beginners to hit their first outdoor shots.

53
Bob Toski

In the mid-1990s, shortly before Leslie King died, we were contacted by a representative of legendary American golf coach, Bob Toski.

He told us that Bob would soon be making his first-ever trip to the British Isles and that the one person he would be most honoured to meet above the Queen or the Prime Minister, would be Leslie King.

Unfortunately, due to Mr King's ill health, he was unable to meet Bob, but we did, and spent an afternoon in Surrey watching him teach.

We had a long chat with him and he told us how much he admired and respected Leslie King. He also found it fascinating that two similar teaching philosophies had grown up entirely independently on either side of the Atlantic.

Jim Flick is another teacher of legendary status and a close associate of Bob's and they have worked extensively together over the years. Jim is also a fan of Leslie King and with technology making the world a smaller place, we frequently see him on our TV screens extolling the virtues of our old master's teaching.

He particularly admired Mr King's instance on training and perfecting a controlled shape through the finish and often refers to how Leslie King built Juli Inkster's swing from front to back!

Sadly, Mr King never did meet either Bob or Jim but we are grateful for their tributes and acknowledgements to the work of Leslie King.

54

Brucie's Bollinger Elbow

Bruce Forsyth has always been the 'King of the Catchphrase'. Think of the legendary entertainer and you can't help but think of "Nice to see you, to see you... nice!", "Didn't he do well?" and, more recently, "Don't tell anyone, but you're my favourite."

Ask Bruce for his favourite, however, and his answer may surprise you. He may just choose one which was coined for him, rather than by him.

Brucie met his match when he came to see Leslie King for golf lessons in the late 1960s. "He gave me the once-over, and looked some more, and snorted and said: 'Bollinger elbow'," recalls Bruce, a self-avowed golf nut. "That's how he described my flying right elbow. I've always struggled with it. Those words still make me smile today. We had a lot of laughs – Mr King made golf fun. What a great teacher he was – and a lovely human being."

Bruce was not the only visitor to get his own special catchphrase. When Amateur Champion Michael Bonallack lifted and tilted his hips on the backswing, King would tell him: "All you need is a grass skirt and you'd be ready for the London Palladium."

Get too much wrist break and he'd tell you to stop waving your club about as if it were VE Day at the end of World War II. Overswing and he'd tell you: "You're heading for an early funeral – go any further and you'll decapitate yourself."

He was just as frank with the ladies. Political correctness, of course, did not exist back then. At least, it did not exist for Leslie King. "Come on, push your rump in," he'd say, if the unfortunate woman in question failed to drive her lower body through impact. "Come on – you've got enough rump to knock down a block of flats."

RIGHT
Two great entertainers, Bruce Forsyth and 'Supermex' Lee Trevino.

55

Gary Player

Throughout his long teaching career, Leslie King enjoyed a good relationship with one of golf's true legends, Gary Player. We believe they met whilst Mr King was teaching fellow South African Harold Henning.

Henning consulted Leslie King throughout his playing career and won two South African Opens, four South African Masters and a host of tour victories. In 1965, he partnered Gary Player to a World Cup win.

Gary Player was a golfer deeply admired by Mr King, and to him was an example of how all professionals should conduct themselves. He admired his manners and his behaviour on and off the course, no matter how he was playing.

He also admired Gary's positive mental approach, his dedication to practice and to fitness and predicted that he would be the blueprint for the tournament player of future generations.

Over the years, the two would regularly meet up at the Open and Gary was most keen to hear Mr King's opinion as to the state of his golf swing. Never more so than in 1974, when having already secured the US Masters, Gary travelled to Royal Lytham & St Annes determined to add the coveted British Open Championship to his Masters triumph.

That week they spent many hours on the practice ground, working together on Gary's swing. Gary was keen for Mr King to stay on for the rest of the week as he was striking the ball and playing so well. Although keen to stay, Mr King explained that he had a full book of lessons at the school to attend. He had a commitment to his regular pupils so sadly would have to return to London. This was typical of the man, as he really felt he couldn't let his pupils down.

Gary went on to win the Championship that year and, to this day, still remembers Mr King fondly. In his own words Leslie King "was one of the greatest students of the golf swing ever."

56

9 out of 10 golfers treat the follow through as an afterthought

...and fail to understand its crucial role in driving the ball towards the target

If you don't think you do, record yourself on video, replay it and think again!

It is not enough to just hit the ball. The ball must be driven forwards. To do this, your hands, arms, body, legs and hips must be travelling through the ball in unison. The arms are extended, though not stretched. The hips are fully turned, the hands maintain control of the clubhead and it remains square in relation to the body.

Front end therapy (pages 119–121) will show you how to replicate the swings of the pros and at last give you a feeling of swinging through the ball rather than hitting at it. Make no mistake, without it you will severely limit your chances of improving.

57

Finishing school

The follow through and finish are integral parts of the swing which do not entirely look after themselves even though the backswing and downswing have been well carried out.

The ball at impact spreads on the face of the club as it is compressed by the momentum of the clubhead at, and just after, impact. Therefore, any deviation or impediment of the clubhead in the follow through will affect the flight of the ball when it parts company with the clubface.

It is frequently claimed that the follow through and finish reflect what has taken place in the earlier stages of the swing. True enough, up to a point, but many a shot has been ruined by a fault being allowed to creep in after impact.

I often hear even an experienced and competent player remark after a shot has been mishit: "I wasn't sure I'd clubbed myself correctly. I quit on the shot for fear of going through the green." In his case the backswing and downswing may well have been perfectly executed. The shot fell below 100% solely because he slightly broke the power and, with it, the control as the clubhead went through the ball – or even before.

The clubhead flies through the hitting area (that part of the arc six inches each side of the ball) in a fraction of a split second. And any irresolution or subconscious inclination to ease off on the shot frequency begins to take effect before the player realises it.

Leslie King, 1961

RIGHT
Faults that occur through the hitting area often begin before impact... with disasterous results.

The follow through is not an afterthought. It must be learnt, understood and committed to muscle memory.

58

An interesting comparison

Pros

Here we can see an unusual, but informative, series of photographs that show the enormous difference between the impact positions of the tour player and the average golfer.

At impact, the tour player has turned the lower body into the shot, creating room for the hands and arms to drive the ball towards the target. The entire body is moving in unison, creating tremendous force in the direction of the ball's intended destination. The poor amateur's position is very different. It is static and lifeless.

Amateurs

These pictures could quite easily have been taken at address. In this case they are not and are the positions that 9 out of 10 golfers find themselves in at impact. Again, we must stress, these are not special cases. All of these golfers have handicaps and hit many a fine shot – from time to time. Rest assured, they will never, ever achieve a sustained improvement unless they master, and commit to muscle memory, this most important part of our programme for immediate improvement.

59

A day in the life of the Knightsbridge Golf School

The video images of the players featured on the opposite page were taken one morning in May 2009.

They are not mock ups. They are genuine golfers with handicaps ranging from 26 to 8. The improvements shown in the second series of printouts were achieved by using a routine that has been employed by the school since the 1950s. Leslie King christened this 'front end therapy' and for many years it was the first thing that a student learnt to do as they built or corrected their golf swing.

Back in golf's black and white days, before visual technology changed players' perception of their swings, it helped thousands achieve an immediate improvement in their standard of play. Up until the introduction of the video camera, students simply did not believe they were in contorted positions, nor did they accept the total lack of control they had in their backswings. If you told them what they did in their swings, they wouldn't believe you. Any backswing change initially feels awkward and the student would argue and say that they couldn't make that backswing change or infer that the teacher had got his analysis wrong.

Leslie King was aware of this and knew that whilst concentrating on the backswing and feeling really awkward, a player would totally black out as he swiped at the ball, with disastrous results. His performance on the course would be so bad that he would simply give up on making the backswing change.

With this in mind he devised 'front end therapy'. By briefly outlining and using a short backswing and concentrating on the hand, arm and body movement through the ball, a player would at least make firm contact with the ball and feel an immediate improvement in his shot-making. If he then played the course using his old backswing with the new follow through he would, to some extent, limit the damage caused by the backswing. In a way this is how some good natural players get away with bad mannerisms in the backswing. Their in-built natural ability somehow senses its way to an acceptable line and movement through the follow through.

Leslie King would make his pupils practise this for a number of weeks until he was confident that they were confident before moving on to re-shaping the backswing.

Writing this in 2009, it still seems a little unusual and revolutionary that a swing could be built back to front, or front to back come to think of it!

But it did work. We built swings like this ourselves. We saw the results with our own eyes and are still seeing it to this day. When pupils from the 1960s and 70s come in for a refresher or a trip down memory lane, their movement through the ball is outstanding and their shot-making all the better for it!

60

Front end therapy will erase this shape forever

STEVE

BEFORE   AFTER

CHESTER

BEFORE   AFTER

DENNIS

BEFORE   AFTER

...ensuring crisp accurate iron shots and adding 50 yards to your drive

Front end therapy exercise

1. Take your address and swing the club into the takeaway, making sure you keep the wrist angle constant and the face of the club square.

2. Swing the club into the ball making sure your right knee, foot and hips are turning into the ball.

4. At hip height the hands and arms run in line with the right hip. Your head now begins to turn towards the target.

5. At the completion of the swing, the body has turned completely towards the target.

3. Keeping your head centred, continue turning the lower body into the target. The hands and arms are moving into the finish, whilst keeping their radius from the body.

6. Finally, drop the arms to hip height and check that the face of the club is square, as it was at address and should have remained throughout the entire swing.

61

Don't kid yourself – your swing is as bad as these!

As you work your way through this book and study the pictures of our featured amateurs, you may think that these players are what we would class as 'extreme cases'. You might reassure yourself that your own swing couldn't possibly be as bad as these lost souls. The reason for this is that you hardly ever see still photographs of amateur golfers.

While you see these swings in motion every time you visit the golf course or driving range, the only still photos you are ever likely to see are of perfectly positioned touring pros in newspapers and magazines.

When an amateur's swing is caught in a still frame it clearly illustrates how poor their swings can be. Rest assured, the players photographed in this book are no worse than the average golfer, or even you. So don't kid yourself. While your swing could be a little better than our models, it could quite easily be a lot worse. Never forget that where you think you are in your swing is hardly ever where you actually are.

62

There are many experts in golf, some even have a handicap

Why are there so many experts in golf? We are not talking about tour teachers, mind gurus and fitness coaches. We are talking about those experts who can't even play to a good standard themselves, but nonetheless feel the need to impose their expertise on others.

We have lost count of the number of times our fledging pupils and even our low handicap players have been derailed from the programme we have laid down for them by some idiotic piece of advice from experts such as these.

When we set to work on a pupil's swing we have a clear idea of where we are taking them. Every piece of the swing is built with utmost care and each part blends effortlessly into the next. When the swing is complete the body, arms, legs and feet are working in total unison – allowing the hands to swing the club through the perfect arc that creates the swing's DNA. The end product is complete and the swing is built as a whole.

No sustained improvement can be attained by using odd tips and pieces of advice like: "keep your head down", "lift the foot up", "pull your

arms down" etc. It is these tips that ruin so many golf swings.

All golfers are at risk from these experts and their 'golden' tips, even those at the very pinnacle of the professional game. Later on in the book we'll look in detail at Seve Ballesteros and the struggle he had with his swing during the latter days of his career. It seems ridiculous but, during that time, he received hundreds of letters and messages from the general public who were convinced that they knew the reason for his malaise and that their particular golden tip would miraculously elevate Seve back to his previous best.

A regular pupil of ours, Glenn Ralph, was a successful tour player during the 1980s and 90s and generally regarded, by his peers, as one of the purest strikers on tour. If Glenn had had a better short game and mental approach to match we believe he could well have become a household name. Nonetheless a couple of years ago, during a Pro-Am, he was also subject to the opinions of one of these experts.

Glenn had played faultless golf through the first nine, scoring an eagle, three

> (Don't be tempted to drag your development off course with a throwaway remark from someone who has never studied your swing)

birdies and five pars to reach the turn in five under. On the 10th tee the chap he was playing with turned to Glenn and said "you would hit it a lot further if you had more wrist break at the top of the backswing, let me give you some help." Glenn could not believe his ears. His prospective teacher had had an air shot on the 1st tee and holed out for an eight. He topped the ball all the way up the 2nd and 3rd and lost three balls through the 4th to 9th holes. His outward total amounted to a princely fifty-two strokes! This is a true story and, rest assured, not an isolated case. Many tour players have similar stories to tell.

Glenn, of course, paid no attention to the ramblings of this seriously deluded expert and has since gone on to have a very successful career on the European Seniors Tour. But for the average player, and especially the beginner, the opinions of these experts are a downright nuisance.

No one suffers this more than the attractive lady golfer. These poor women are frequently subject to the attention of these experts whenever they go to a busy driving range or practice ground.

Even though they may be working conscientiously and correctly on their swings, it is never too long before their swings are subject to the unwanted advice of the self-proclaimed experts. Thankfully, due to being prior warned by us, our pupils know better than to listen to these characters, but in the past many fine fledging swings have been severely damaged.

Husbands and boyfriends also do their best to interfere with our work and their advice is just as damaging as the guys at the range who, in all honesty, are just trying to chat them up!

So, what can be done about these experts? We'd like to say we have a solution but unfortunately we have no idea. All we can do is warn you, in the strongest possible terms, about the dangers of their golden tips and how they can seriously affect your swing model. Instead think through your swing as a whole, consider how everything works together – don't be tempted to drag your development off course with a throwaway remark from someone who has never studied your swing.

63

Our time on tour

We first met Stephen Ames towards the end of the 1995 season at St Mellion in Cornwall. Stephen had what, to the casual observer, looked to be a fine swing. However, to our eyes, there was far too much wrist action in the backswing. With his driver the shaft would frequently drop well below the horizontal, causing inconsistency off the tee and a lack of accuracy with his irons. We did a little work with him that week and the following spring he called us, saying that he'd like to do a little more, and asked if it would be possible to fly over for a bit of a lesson. For the first and only time, and against the strictest rules of our lease, we opened the school on a Sunday afternoon and took Stephen through his swing, showing him, in great detail, how destructive the excessive wrist movement was. We also worked on keeping a better balance through impact and into the finish.

Over the next few weeks we took him to Stoke Park and in May accompanied him to the country's first event of the season, the Benson & Hedges International, held at the Oxfordshire. The week didn't start well. The wind was howling and gathering strength, and the airline had somehow misplaced his golf clubs. Monday morning was spent hanging around a freezing practice ground cursing the airline and waiting for the clubs to turn up. By mid-afternoon they were finally delivered and the remainder of the afternoon was spent reiterating what we had taught Stephen in the school. We worked hard on his swing that week and by the start of play had taken a huge chunk off his backswing.

Conditions were poor. A fifty mile-an-hour freezing wind made good golf almost impossible and players dropped shots wholesale as they vainly struggled to somehow keep the ball in play. Stephen,

> Though we can in no way claim credit for his current success, we honestly believe that Stephen's swing is now better and stronger than ever

however, was unaffected. His new compact action more than stood up to the conditions and by Sunday evening he was crowned Benson & Hedges International champion.

A few years later Stephen left the European tour to make his name in the United States. He is now quite rightly recognised as one of the leading players on the US tour and in 2006 won the Tournament Players championship, generally regarded as golf's fifth major. Though we can in no way claim credit for his current success, we honestly believe that his swing is now better and stronger than ever and he will stay at the top of his game for many years to come.

Another fine young professional we had the pleasure to work with was David Carter, who visited us shortly after recovering from a life-saving operation to relieve pressure on the brain caused by a mystery virus. David had been only hours from death when his colleague alerted Saudi hotel staff who battered his bedroom door open to find him unconscious.

We first met David some eighteen months beforehand, whilst working with Stephen Ames. After recovering from his ordeal, he made his way to Knightsbridge as he felt he needed a little guidance on his technique. His swing was essentially good, but he suffered a slight backswing wrist roll which led to a little inconsistency and lack of distance with both wood and iron. After a few sessions at the school and at Stoke Park he felt a great improvement in his ball striking and a few months later defeated Colin Montgomery in a play-off to win the Irish Open at Druids Glen. A few months after that he partnered Sir Nick Faldo to victory in golf's World Cup. David is still a tour regular at the time of writing and we have pleasant memories of teaching this polite, well-grounded and down-to-earth professional.

64

Sandy and Seve

During our time on tour, our one big regret was not getting the chance to help two players who we deeply believe could have benefited from our tuition. Sandy Lyle and Seve Ballesteros were young talents, recognised by Leslie King as having enormous potential. D.J. has been at the School since 1970 and was party to Leslie King's observations of their precocious talent. Whilst teaching Michael King, a leading amateur of the time, Mr King was with the Great Britain and Ireland Walker Cup Team and singled out a young protégé who he recommended team members to study. According to Mr King, the young Sandy Lyle had the most beautiful of golf swings. He was strong, had a great tempo and a first class technique.

A few years later Leslie King again had the opportunity to observe Lyle's swing at close quarters and showed a little concern as a slight twist of his hands and wrists started to appear in the backswing. At the time this slight twist of the wrist held no problems for Lyle and he went on to enjoy a brilliantly successful career. However, as the years went by, the slight hitch in Sandy's backswing started to get more and more exaggerated and, by the mid-nineties, Sandy had really started to struggle. To us, the source of his problems was obvious, as we'd

been told about it before it even started to affect him. He tried many different tactics, tried changing different areas of the swing, but nothing made any difference to his consistency. Meanwhile, the wrist twist remained exactly the same as it had always been – unaltered and still the source of all his problems.

Sandy was once interviewed by a leading broadsheet and quizzed on his relative demise. His reply was typical of many a naturally gifted professional:

"When I was good, I didn't know what I was doing and when I was bad, I didn't know what I was doing."

A similar story can be told about Seve Ballesteros, another great player whose success, it is generally believed, came to an end far too prematurely. As with Sandy Lyle, Leslie King paid close attention to Seve's emerging talent and studied him at close hand – particularly when he came over for the Open Championship, in the long hot summer of 1976. For younger readers, it is probably worth explaining that Seve Ballesteros was unquestionably the Tiger Woods of his day. He had enormous talent, oozed charisma and was the name on everyone's lips. He hit the ball a country

mile, played remarkable recovery shots and had a fantastic short game. Brooding good looks and a cavalier attitude completed the package. He was the real deal.

Ballesteros finished joint second in that Open and three years later became the first Spaniard to win the same event. He won it again in 1984 and 1988, collected two Masters titles and achieved legendary status.

Years afterwards, a slight, previously imperceptible, mannerism started to become more and more exaggerated. Slowly but surely it began to affect his performance. The fault in itself was connected with his hand line on the backswing. As documented many times in this book, a twist or roll of the hands on the backswing is the constant enemy of all golfers, even Sandy Lyle. But this was something a little more complicated.

Not only did the wrist begin to roll, it also picked up and screwed in at the same time. Leslie King saw the early signs of this developing fault many years before. He put this down to the hours of practice Seve had spent perfecting his tricky little chip shots from around the green and told us that if this hand movement worked its way into his full swing, he would be in trouble. So it came to pass and Seve never recaptured his previous form, despite no want of trying. He worked with many tour teachers, yet none could clean up his backswing hand line. Everyone gave him advice but no one got anywhere near making an impression on the faulty action. But we felt we could have. At the time we'd had a combined forty years teaching experience and had learnt from Leslie King's sixty-

showed him how his hands should look at each and every stage of the takeaway, as described elsewhere in this book. As his hand line became cleaner, he could once again feel the beautiful left arm leverage that he had in his early days.

This had been lost in an earlier attempt to change his swing. His shoulder tilt had been correctly taken out, but unfortunately he had lost his arm leverage in the process. This short backswing, combined with the poor hand movement, had made things even worse. In our company, though, he could, for the first time in years, feel his arm leverage again. From the top of the backswing, we swung his arms up and down and once more he could now feel his line into the ball. The next day we saw him on TV and he was practising the drills we had shown him. We are certain that it was no coincidence that he made four or five consecutive cuts over the next few weeks.

So what happened? Why didn't we continue seeing him and why did he never contact us? Well, shortly afterwards we left the tour to concentrate on our clientele and, as mentioned previously, he probably thought we were no different to the other teachers trying to gain a reputation as tour coaches. His golf deteriorated as his swing gradually crept back to its old ways – poor hand line, lack of leverage – and he tried something else. Today, it's doubtful he would even remember us. We were just teachers passing through, but we honestly believe that, given a few weeks, we could

year experience and his observations on the origin of Seve's error.

In all fairness, we did have our day in the sun. Well, half an hour to be exact. Whilst teaching on tour Seve called us over to see what we thought of his swing. Although this may sound encouraging, at that time he had been interested in what countless teachers had to say. Hundreds of people had given him advice. Articles had appeared in newspapers and magazines, and numerous people had written to him claiming to know the secret of his sorrow. He probably perceived us as no more than another couple of faceless tour teachers.

However we know that in that half hour we had begun to make inroads into eradicating the evil triple movement in his hands. We went through the backswing as we always do in super slow motion and

> Experience is not spending years on tour teaching the supremely talented; experience is working day after day, year after year, with the average golfer – the typical reader of this book

have secured a massive improvement.

Someone we did manage to help was Seve's fellow countryman, Miguel Martin. Miguel had struggled for a long time and with only a few weeks of the season to go, was in serious danger of losing his tour card. We first met him on the practice ground, surrounded by what was known at the time as 'The Spanish Armada', including Jimenez, Olazabal and a couple of others. Everyone was offering Miguel different bits of advice. Of course, none of it made any difference and he looked to us in total despair.

The trouble? You guessed it. He was twisting his hands and wrists on the takeaway! As we gave our analysis, the Armada shook their heads, stifled a few guffaws and awaited our embarrassment. Of course they didn't realise that we'd been teaching tour golf a lot longer than they'd been playing tour golf. As expected, following a method tried and tested in tens of thousands of lessons, Miguel immediately got the message. This is the great thing about teaching magically talented professionals with God-given hands. Once they are shown the correct hand line, they can immediately feel how the perfect hand line allows them to feel the correct line back into the ball.

Miguel felt that a great weight had been lifted from his shoulders. As shot after shot sailed down the centre of the practice ground, the Spanish Armada looked down, shook their heads and muttered under their breath. It was hard not to laugh as their initial disdain turned into a haughty exit; rarely on the European Tour has the legendary Latin temperament been in fuller evidence.

As Miguel worked his way through hitting mid-irons and woods, he looked up, smiled and said: "two iron". This was the acid test: The Hardest Club in the Bag. Miguel knew that if he could do it with a two iron, his salvation was complete. The ball shot forwards, long and low, ate up the ground and finished a good twenty yards further than he had been accustomed to.

We saw Miguel on many occasions after that but only briefly, as the work that was done that day proved almost enough. He easily regained his tour card and the following season secured enough points to earn a Ryder Cup place. He never actually played in the team due to a controversial set of circumstances, too unusual and detailed to go into here, but went on to enjoy a very successful career, as did we when we returned to Knightsbridge, to the warmth of our everyday clients.

65

The beginner
A case history

When I first started taking lessons I didn't even know how to hold a club and was warned not to interfere with the method I was learning. I thought that sounded a little over-the-top and almost arrogant. Surely there must be some other people on the planet that can pass on some golfing wisdom? Looking back, I wouldn't count on it.

After my first series of lessons with Steve, he was still wary about me going off on golfing holidays, engaging in some unsupervised DIY. You could argue that it wasn't really unsupervised; my so-called expert was my boyfriend who has been playing 'good' golf for the last ten years. Before I left Steve, he repeated to me over and over again not to take advice from anyone. My promise was as big as it had been when I joined the Hungarian Girl Scouts aged seven.

Finally unleashed onto the golf course, I started hitting some really good shots, easy and light and dead straight. My only problem was that they weren't going quite as far as I would have liked. But I had made a promise to Steve and I would keep it. I was determined not be seduced by the mystery of clubhead speed.

I failed! Neither of us could resist the temptation. My boyfriend had to start telling me what to do differently (boyfriends just want the best for you, right?) and I had to at least try it out. Surely Steve would not notice and may even be impressed. At this point I made another promise, this time to myself: I would not tell him about it.

Back in Knightsbridge, it took only one shot and Steve was on my case. "Who has been messing with MY golf swing?" he exclaimed. I was taken aback; one swing, one look and he knew. So at that point I had to break my second promise and own up to him. He was right. As the video proved, my backswing went far too far back and I finished off nicely with a 'crispy chicken wing' at the follow through. You might think 'What's the big fuss about?', but it took me the best part of five lessons to get my original swing back – and, more importantly, my confidence. Now that I am spending more time with low handicap golfers, I refuse to take advice from them. If something does not work, I would rather call Steve on his cell phone (even on a Sunday) describing my problems than listen to the so-called experts around me.

Thanks to both of you Steve and Dave and I am very, very sorry for doubting you!
Patricia Szarvas

66

The ball must be driven forwards

1

2

3

1. Hip Height Finish

Post-impact, the swing must maintain its controlled shape. The hips should continue to turn into the finish and – most crucially – the arms should retain their distance from the body, with the clubface remaining square. The arms should not have splayed, nor should the wrists have collapsed or crossed over.

2. Shoulder height finish

At shoulder height the left arm should have folded downwards. The hands and wrists will appear slightly convexed. The face of the club should remain square in relation to the body.

3. The full finish

At the full finish the hip turn is complete. The right foot is up on its toes, the left leg is straight and the arm swing is complete. Always make a point of holding the finish until after the ball has landed, as this will reinforce the feeling of swinging through the ball rather than at the ball.

The shoulder height finish

Above are three perfect examples of correct hand and arm positions at the shoulder height finish. The right arm is straight, the left arm has folded and the arms are close together. The left wrist is concave and the right slightly convex.

At shoulder height the arms are naturally extended and the elbows are close together. It is only after this that the elbows give as the swing completes the full finish.

67

Connected

The hands, arms and body must be connected and working together in unison throughout the entire swing. The following exercise will give you the feeling of connection throughout the finish.

Hold the club at the bottom of the grip and place the shaft into your belt buckle. Lean over into your address position and then simply turn the body into a half-finish whilst keeping the shaft connected to your body.

This exercise is an excellent way to promote the feeling of connection and protects against any splaying of the elbows through impact, which causes a blocked shot to the right or, if the ball has moved forwards, an embarrassing lack of distance. The elbows splaying through the impact area and finish can also be blamed for the topped shot.

Remember, the finish must not be overlooked. The ball must be driven forwards and to do this a structured modelled finish is essential.

Faultless Finish

1. At impact the clubface is square, the head centre, the right knee has folded towards the target as the hips have turned.

2. At hip height the arms are almost in line with the right hip as the right knee and hip continues to turn into the finish. The left hand is concave as it was on the backswing, and the right hand is slightly convex.

3. At shoulder height the hands and arms are in line with the left shoulder and the hips have almost completed their turn.

These faultless positions can be copied by any golfer, regardless of age or ability. However, it is important to understand once again that the movements must be learnt in slow motion, one piece at a time.

68

Golfer's elbow

We are all aware of the term 'tennis elbow' and the various treatments and painful cortisone injections that go with it. However what we have more concern with is the lesser known, but equally uncomfortable, golfer's elbow. Unlike tennis elbow, golfer's elbow is found in the left arm and is generally caused by one of three reasons.

Driving range mats of old were notorious for causing golfer's elbow. The hard rubber mat sat on a solid concrete base has claimed many victims. The constant jarring on the arm as the club made contact with the ball and ground sent the trauma up the arm and onto the elbow.

Thankfully, these days driving range mats are much better and the artificial surface generally gives a little as the club goes into the back of the ball. It can, however, still be a problem and even practising on a hard grass surface can cause golfer's elbow, as experienced a few years ago by Sir Nick Faldo.

If you frequently practise on ranges, are suffering a pain in the left arm and suspect this could be the reason for your problem, get your own tee and cut it down so that the ball sits just above the surface. This could well preserve your elbow's health.

Poor technique is also responsible for golfer's elbow. In the first instance a bent left arm on the backswing must be considered. If the arm jumps as it straightens on the downswing, the pressure will be pushed onto the elbow joint. The cure is to keep the left arm straight, though not stiff, throughout the backswing and start down. To practice this go through the backswing slowly. Stop at the top and swing the club down to waist height. Tee the ball up and hit shots practicing this drill in slow motion. As you get used to the feeling of the backswing, gradually increase your speed and very shortly you should have cured your elbow and improved your swing.

The third and final cause of golfer's elbow can be found in the delivery of the clubhead to and through the ball. If your right hand overtakes your left during impact, the pressure will be forced onto the left elbow joint. If you continue to play like this you will gradually put more and more stress onto the elbow joint and inevitably golfer's elbow will follow. The cure, once again, is to look to the swing's basics and learn how to deliver the clubhead with the hands, arms and body working in unison through to a hip height finish.

As with golfer's back, sound swing basics and mastery of the swing's DNA should ensure good golfing health. Remember that a good swing is effortless, strain free and places no undue strain onto

69

Head up!

'Head up' is one of the oldest clichés in golf and something the poor old teaching pro would tell his pupil if he wasn't really sure what had caused his student's bad shot.

Head up, of course, means lifting the head prior to impact, thus destroying the contact with the ball.

So where does head up come from and what causes the head to lift up just before impact? The answer is our old adversary – the reflex. The reflex is responsible for the subconscious urge to hit the ball prematurely. Once the reflex has flared, the eyes and, consequently, the head, lift up to follow the ball. The solution to the head up problem lies in learning to control the reflex and learning to make a swing through the ball, rather than trying to hit at it.

70

Surely there's more than one way to skin a cat?

When we first started teaching, back in the 1970s, there were many individualistic swings on the professional tour. Players such as Lee Trevino, Doug Sanders, Ray Floyd and a host of others all employed their own individual and very effective actions. These days such swings are very much in the minority and 90% of tour pros share the same basics that you are being taught in this book – and with very good reason. The simpler the swing, the simpler it is to repeat each and every time. The better each swing position is, and subsequent swing stage is, the easier it is to deliver the clubhead consistently to the ball. Although players such as Jim Furyk, John Daly and Fred Couples may have unconventional

backswings they all return to an orthodox position by the time they have entered the hitting area, prior to delivering the clubhead into the ball. They have to be, as the only way a golf ball can be driven forwards is by the club approaching the ball from the inside, to a long square apex at impact, before returning to the inside at the quarter finish.

In thirty-five years we have rarely met an amateur who could compensate to such a degree on the downswing that he could continue to use a badly flawed backswing. Unless you are extremely talented, which unfortunately excludes most of us, your only way forward is to 'clean up' your backswing by learning the backswing hand line, the master key to good golf.

Once the backswing has been committed
to muscle memory, all conscious thought
can return to delivering the clubhead to the
ball – the essence of an effective golf swing.
To stand on the tee knowing that your
backswing is 100% sound and that your only
thoughts are on striking the ball squarely is a
fantastic feeling, usually only experienced by
the gifted natural golfer.

Jim Furyk's swing has cruelly been
compared to an octopus falling out of a
tree! It is only in the backswing, however,
that Furyk's swing varies from the ideal. By
the time he has entered the hitting area his
positions are totally orthodox. As he hits the
ball and moves into the quarter finish his
position is that of every other great player
featured in this book.

71

Gianfranco Zola

One of us is a huge fan of Chelsea FC. Not one of the prawn sandwich brigade, but someone who has been going to Stamford Bridge all his life, not to mention Rotherham and similarly glamorous venues to watch some of the most miserable drubbings in the club's history. So you can imagine his reaction when, one day in the summer of 1997, probably the most talented player in Chelsea's history popped his head around the golf school's door. We've met some very famous and important people in our time, but for the first time ever 'Mr Celebrity Golf Teacher' was flummoxed and his clipped West London accent was temporarily replaced by a rather confusing form of gibberish.

When the power of speech eventually returned, he enquired as to Franco's golfing history and was told that he'd recently taken up the game and found it a little more demanding than football, to say the least. Thankfully, the time we spent with Franco resulted in him getting down to a 7 handicap and becoming totally obsessed with the game.

However, if you think that he was a natural and easy to teach, we can assure you this was far from the truth. In fact, he was one of our least coordinated pupils of the time. He even had the distinction of smashing a plate glass mirror directly behind him as he rolled the club into the backswing: a mirror that had stood proudly intact for nearly fifty years! He also

lacked the control in his feet to perform the trick of teeing the ball up by holding it between his right foot and his 5 iron – a skill that we had long since mastered!

It was his work ethic alone that helped him improve. He worked hard and then worked harder. He also showed an intensity of understanding, study and application that we frequently see in those who are at the very top of their chosen profession.

As you'd expect, the public face of Franco is the private face of Franco, and though it's been said many times before, we have to add that he really is the perfect gentleman.

He was also keen to settle his tuition bills, and on one occasion, invited us over to his apartment as he'd forgotten his chequebook and was determined to pay us promptly. We couldn't get over there quick enough and it certainly felt somewhat surreal being waited on with coffee and biscuits by a man who at least one (and, by now, probably both) of us idolised.

When he eventually became the best golfer at Chelsea he finally decided to reveal his secret golfing tuition to his team mates. When Gianluca Vialli pitched up for his first lesson, he told us that he'd wanted to come to us for ages, but Franco hadn't told him how to contact us until he had got significantly better than him. Which shows how competitive these great sportsmen really are – even when the sport in question isn't their chosen career.

Along with Franco and Luca we have met and taught many footballers

including Carlo Cudicini, Frank McLintock, Ray Houghton and the late, great Peter Osgood to name but a few. Contrary to the bad press that footballers suffer, we have found them to be a lot easier to deal with than their golfing professional counterparts! Maybe this is because football is a team game, rather than the necessarily self-obsessed world of the professional golf tour.

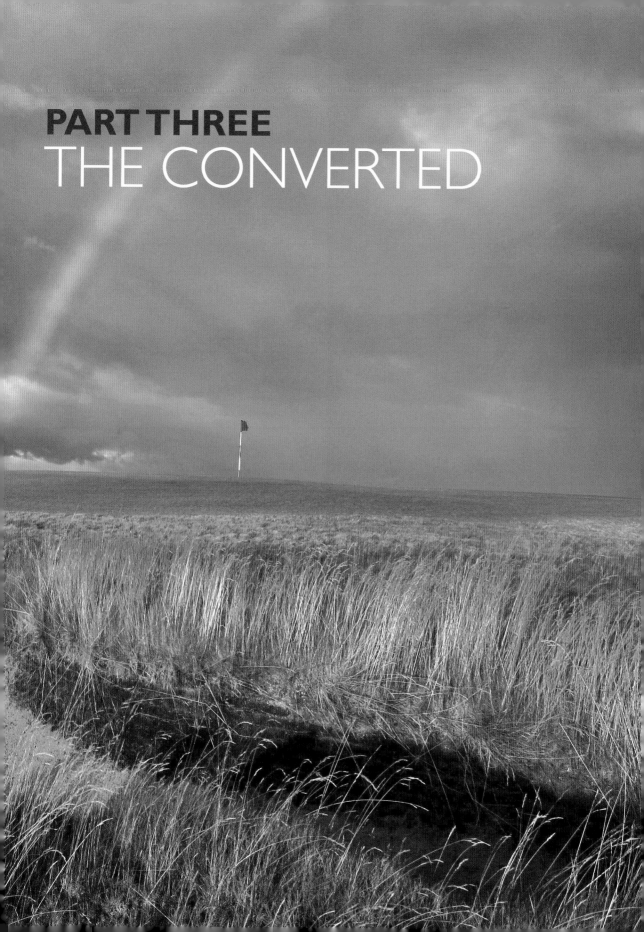

PART THREE
THE CONVERTED

72

You don't have to be a sportsman

Left-handers cause us no problems whatsoever.

Golf is different from other games. Natural ball players are not necessarily good at golf and those that haven't got natural ball sense can actually excel. This is due to the fact that golf is a dead ball game. In almost all other ball sports, with the exception of snooker, pool and croquet, you need to have a quick reflex and get to the ball before it gets past you. This is the total opposite to golf, where the reflex must be suppressed until the club is delivered to and through the ball. The idea of hitting at the ball is totally alien to good golfing technique.

For years people believed that left-handers were a special case and had more problems with their swings. We have never found this to be true. The only problem they really had was getting hold of some decent

clubs, as their choice was very limited. We have always taught a fair number of left-handers and they cause us no problems whatsoever. The triumphs of left-handers Mike Weir and Phil Mikelson at Masters tournaments in 2003, 2004 and 2006 certainly validates the point.

Golfers with disabilities can also be taught our swing model. Over the years we have had many such golfers and at the moment we are teaching a girl with a prosthetic right leg and a man who is registered blind.

One-armed golfers can reach a very high standard but those who only have their right arm fare a lot better than those with their left. Right arm players tend to move through the ball far more powerfully and to have greater control.

73

A tale of two golfers
part one

It's a typical Tuesday morning and two beginners are being pushed and pulled through the basic swing shapes that have been taught at the school for over sixty years.

In the far bay we have a vision, a beautiful girl in her mid-twenties who we shall call 'Katie'. She goes through her pre-shot routine, checks her appearance in the mirror, adjusts her designer polo shirt, flicks a curl behind her ear and draws the club back to the top of the backswing. She pauses momentarily before delivering the clubhead firmly and squarely into the back of the ball. With a sharp crack it dissects the centre of the net. At the finish she is pro-like, drops her arms to hip height and checks the club face. Needless to say it is square. A truly wonderful sight, a natural beauty and a carefully constructed golf swing that is so fluid and graceful that it looks as natural as its owner.

In the other bay stands a familiar face, a study of concentration, a look we have seen many times before, usually prior to dispatching the ball high into the top left hand corner of the net. This man is intense, the consummate professional. Throughout his career he has stayed long after training perfecting the dead ball technique that along with his tricks and twists and god-given genius has made him somewhat of a legend to his adoring fans. It is now, however, a very different dead ball that he is standing over: a lot smaller and a lot more intimidating. He is the perfect pupil, he listens intently to his teacher and solemnly works his way through the basic swing shapes. His new swing has now reached maturity. Shot after shot flies into the middle of the net and he knows he is now ready to take his game to the golf course.

In reception, a lavishly tattooed young man is deep in conversation with an elegant, titled lady in her seventies. They have both recently taken up the game, are mid-way through their first series of lessons and are considering which of their friends they should contact to accompany them to the practice range.

Let's now return to our two fore-mentioned pupils and step three months into the future. The venue has changed. We are now on the lush fairways of Stoke Park, the School's second home, our country residence. The 5th hole plays host to our Premiership superstar. He is going along quite nicely. There is no scorecard in his pocket; he knows that comes later. All he is concerned with is keeping his swing together, making a good strike and retaining his tempo. If he hits a bad shot it doesn't bother him, he just puts another one down and tries again. He has no score to worry about, he has been taught not to. He knows that he must first learn to strike the ball consistently, add a short game to his

Natalia is a raw beginner. She has learnt her swing indoors under controlled conditions. When these pictures were taken she had played no more than a few games of golf, yet she swings the club as well as any player on tour.

armoury and learn to play the game of golf. Only then can he take his newly learned skills into a competitive battle with the golf course and its scorecard.

As he tees off, he shudders as he recalls his first experience of the dreaded first tee. A man used to performing at the highest level in front of 42,000 spectators reduced to a quivering wreck by a group of established members sipping gin and tonics on the clubhouse balcony, wishing him to fail. They too have been hugely successful in their own fields: a doctor, a scientist and a veteran from a bloody foreign conflict, but they too have been reduced to a bag of nerves by the infamous first tee.

Thankfully, the first tee now holds no fears for our pupil. He trusts his swing, trusts his tempo and the foundations are in place for a lifetime of enjoyable golf.

Meanwhile, on the 17th a very different tale is unfolding. Could it really be Katie we see in the distance? What has happened to this paragon of elegance? The composure

has gone. Great lumps of turf are dug from the fairway, expletives explode from Katie's delicate lips and the ball, if struck at all, shoots right, then left, then right again. Or, as a certain comedian would say, she is playing military golf. The swing is grotesque. What was once so elegant, so simple and so functional is now just a series of tilting hips, dropping shoulders and twisting hands. What has happened to destroy this wonderful golf swing?

Unlike our gentleman footballer, Katie's transition from golf school swot to golf course dunce has taken a very different route. She first went to a driving range with a girlfriend. Within minutes they were surrounded by an endless procession of testosterone-charged golfing experts. A plumber, a roofer and an airline pilot (or at least he said he was). One by one, they offered their wisdom. Take it back further, break your wrists, don't stop at the top of the backswing. Our plumber friend even suggested that a session on his Tiger Woods

PlayStation game would help enormously, adding that he only lived around the corner, so it would be no inconvenience at all! Katie's fate was all but sealed. She hit the mat, missed the ball five times and hit that cursed bay divider twice – which seemed to scream "you're an idiot!" She left the range totally confused. She'd started well but begun to deteriorate immediately after the 'tuition' began. By the end of the session she didn't know her arm from her elbow.

Worse however, was to follow. Her next excursion was to the course itself with her boyfriend; a 6 foot 2 rugger-type, who hit the ball a mile and knew everything. "Katie, put the ball on the ground. You can't tee it up on the fairway," he barks as he launches his own ball screaming down the fairway and deep into the woods. "Katie, hurry! You are holding everybody up! No you can't hit it again; of course you have to take a score! *Remember! Strict rules of golf!*" He quotes from *Goldfinger*, and finds this highly amusing.

However, for Katie it is anything but amusing, and she has become totally disillusioned by the 'game' of golf.

But it could have been so different.

We now return to the school. The teaching bays have two new occupants. Once graduated, our titled lady has arranged a trip to the driving range with our tattooed friend. She is not sure what nu-metal actually is but suspects it has something to do with the recycling industry. She has found her new friend to be an extremely charming young man. Culturally, they are worlds apart but their child-like enthusiasm for their new obsession has drawn together two very unlikely companions. It will soon be time for them to venture outside, but what will the future hold? We'll return to them later.

Katie doesn't play golf any more. She has tried Pilates and has heard that yoga is all the rage again. Our footballing hero plays golf almost everyday and has a low single figure handicap – two contrasting tales.

74

It is impossible to learn golf outside – it just can't be done

This is obviously a ridiculous statement and a long way from the truth. However, look at it another way and you could conclude that it's not so silly after all.

If you go to any driving range or public golf course you will see some truly horrendous sights. The ascent of man really does start here. Ham-fisted grips, contorted body shapes, brute force and ignorance is alive and well at a driving range in your area. However, no blame should be placed on the perpetrators. They know no other way. They have bought the books, read the magazines and may have even had the occasional lesson. Sadly, for these people golf will never be any different. They have come as far as they can – the end of the road.

How did they end up in this dead end and what route took them there? The answer lies in the way they started. The majority first went to the driving range or, worse still, the golf course, with a well-meaning friend eager to introduce them to the magical game of golf. Without any tuition or thought as to what they should be doing, they swish the club back and at the ball and hope that somehow they make contact. The law of averages dictates that with even the most primitive of swings, contact is made with the odd ball and they naïvely believe that a few tips here and there will take the 'rough edges' off their swing, turning two good shots out of fifty into two bad shots out of fifty! The reality is very different. The seeds have been sown for a lifetime of misery. Golf is a precision sport. A good structure is essential and must be learnt under controlled conditions. This is where the indoor experience comes into its own. Indoors the golf swing can be learnt stage by stage, with great care and clarity. A pupil can be guided through the correct positions without the distraction of trying to hit the ball. He can build himself a sound swing structure that creates the hand line of the naturally gifted golfer with God-given hands.

The first thing we build for our pupils is correct body poise. This is an umbrella term we use for the pitch of the body, the shoulder and hip turn and the balance in the legs and feet.

Once this is established, the hands and arms can now learn to swing the club on the correct plane. Our swing model teaches the swing in slow motion segments,

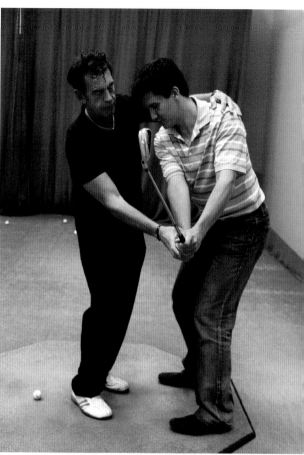

Indoors the golf swing can be learnt stage by stage, with great care and clarity.

building a piece at a time that very quickly become one flowing movement. Only when a pupil is comfortable with their swing do we take them outside to test their skill in the open air.

If you are reading this as a beginner, it is essential that you make yourself comfortable with the swing's DNA before venturing out into the open. Every position in our swing model can be practised anywhere. You don't even need a club. Just link your hands together and go through the movements.

The swing's DNA has to be learnt in exactly the same way as it is for the seasoned player. If anything it is a little

easier for the beginner, as there are no bad habits to break down.

Another great way to learn a swing is to learn the finish first, as described in front end therapy (pages 119–121). It was the way we taught our beginners for years, and even today we are impressed with golfers who first learnt with us many years ago when they return for a check up. Having checked the basic grip and address, simply go through steps 1 to 4 of front end therapy. This should cement in your mind the essential line through the ball at impact and beyond. Tee the ball up, use a short backswing and simply tap the ball into a hip height finish. As your

> (Golf is a precision sport.
> A good structure is essential
> and must be learnt under
> controlled conditions)

confidence grows, take your club back to hip height (ensuring the wrists haven't rolled!) and once again, tap the ball into the hip height finish.

When you can successfully hit the ball consistently down the middle, progress through the three-quarter backswing and eventually to the full backswing, whilst maintaining the hip height finish. This really is a great way to learn a swing and will speed you on your journey to becoming a successful golfer.

In the 1970s a pupil of ours, Stephen Jones, learnt in this way and reached the semi-final of the English Amateur Championship, after having only played golf for eighteen months. From time to time we still see Stephen and his swing shape has hardly changed from the beautiful simple movement we made for him all those years ago.

When you first go to the driving range or practice ground, try to go alone. That way you will be free to practice the swing at your own pace and in your own time. Once again, be warned that if you go with a golfing friend, he or she will not be able to stop themselves giving you their advice and sharing their expertise.

Try not to do too much on your first few visits. A bucket of balls should be sufficient. It is also very important that you tee the ball up. All that matters at this early stage is securing a solid strike.

When first venturing on the course, you should continue teeing the ball up, even on the fairway. This may seem strange, but in the long run will help immensely. When you eventually place the ball on the fairway your swing will be so strong that the ground should hold no fears at all. Before playing your first round of golf, we strongly recommend visiting your local club pro for an introduction to the short game. Putting, of course, can be honed on your living room carpet. Once you have made the transition from driving range to golf course try not to worry too much about posting a decent score. Scores will follow, but the priority must be learning to strike the ball; pitch and putt and generally building yourself a golf game. Never forget the basic DNA of the swing model, the backswing hand line, pre-squaring the club before impact and keeping the club on line through the finish. Whatever you do, don't mess around with your swing, trying this or that latest discovery or teaching gimmick. If you follow this advice you should have all you need to give yourself a solid golf game to last for life.

75

Why we do not give golf day clinics

We are often invited to give a pre-tournament clinic at clients' guest days and corporate events. You know the sort of thing – go around, tweak a few strings and give a few tips. Although these days could prove to be very lucrative, we always refuse the offer.

The reasons are simple. 99% of golfers invited to these events are people we haven't seen before and so have never had a chance to build them a swing. Usually their swings are in such a mess that to start working on their technique just before a competition would be absolute madness.

Conscious thought is the enemy of all golfers and it is totally impossible to play a round of golf whilst thinking consciously on any isolated part of the movement. If, for example, a player is twisting the club on the takeaway, to try and correct the movement would confuse him and make him feel so uncomfortable he would probably miss the ball altogether.

However, if he had been through our programme and had the basic fundamental positions of his swing in place, it would be a different matter altogether. Every Monday we take a group of pupils out to Stoke Park. These students have the fundamentals in place. We can work on their swing knowing they have the basic structure from which their swing can be tweaked to give maximum results.

There is great danger in giving tips and advice to players we haven't seen before and who don't plan to see us in the future. Unbeknownst to us they could be working on a particular plan of instruction with their regular teacher and any intrusive invasion from us may be detrimental to their coach's master plan. This has happened to us on many occasions. A pupil has received advice from a coach that in itself was correct. However, taken out of context with how our pupil was constructing their swing, it was totally misleading.

Here is an example.

A middle-aged lady client had been seeing us for some time. Without wishing to be cruel, it is fair to say that she had no particular flair for the game, had never been a sportsperson and had to work extremely hard to reach a standard that would allow her to enjoy a lifetime of consistent golf. We accompanied her on her first few visits to the Golf Club and eventually felt happy about her gaining her independence.

After a few successful excursions of her own she told us that she'd been invited to play in a Charity Golf Day. We were still

The Knightsbridge Golf School does not give tips and bits of advice, we build golf swings.

a little protective and told her not to take advice from her playing partners – just to stick to what she'd been taught.

The day after the event she came into the school, almost in tears. "I didn't hit one good shot," she said. "I didn't get one airborne. I hit the ground a foot behind the ball. I hit straight out to the right." The poor woman was distraught and she told us the story of what had been a truly dreadful day.

She had taken her place on the practice ground and hit a few shots to loosen up. It's important at this stage to tell you that her flexibility and ability to swing the club freely were not naturally good. With this in mind we allowed her to straighten her right leg a little on the backswing, which gave her a little more freedom than she might otherwise have had. As she loosened up she hit shot after shot down the centre of the practice ground and was feeling rather proud of herself. After about ten minutes a vaguely familiar figure appeared behind her. She wasn't sure where she recognised him from but in retrospect realised that she had seen his face on many of the hundreds of golf magazines that her husband owned.

After introducing himself and engaging in a little small talk, he turned his attention to her swing and was very complimentary about her technique. However, he suggested that she should try to keep her right knee bent on the backswing which in itself, of course, is good technique and has been taught at the school since its inception. But in this instance, with this player's history, this advice proved catastrophic. The poor woman forgot everything else and concentrated solely on her right knee. She lost her shoulder turn, her arm leverage and the hand movement. Unfortunately, this again illustrates the danger, as previously mentioned, in seeing one part of the swing in isolation without consideration of what goes either before or after it, or how a particular pupil has been trained.

Our pupil gradually re-learnt her swing shape and regained the standard she had previously played. But it was all so unnecessary and highlights the reason why we do not participate in the corporate golf day clinic, even though we'd like to help as many golfers as we could.

76

Age at either extreme is no barrier

Senior golfers can sometimes be wary of taking up golf. This is partly because they mistakenly believe that you need to be extremely flexible to create the sort of swing employed by the tour pros. This isn't necessarily so. As long as the shoulders can turn 90 degrees, the hips 45 degrees and the arms be raised above head height, they will have all the flexibility they'll ever need.

Thankfully we are all living a little longer these days. The seventies are the new sixties, and the eighties the new seventies. We have had a great number of pupils who have taken up the game in their eighties. Recently, one senior golfer was very upset when he saw his swing on video. It wasn't, however, his swing that bothered him. It was the bald spot that he had noticed on the back of his head!

At the other end of the scale, children are taking up the game at an ever younger age. Good nutrition is making them stronger earlier and modern golf equipment is so much lighter, allowing them to have better control of the club. When teaching children it is important that control is maintained through both ends of the swing. Care should be taken not to let the club go too far back on the backswing. If the club is allowed to go to horizontal it will, in time, start dipping below the horizontal due to children's hands not being so well developed and therefore lacking a little control. A shoulder height finish is also recommended for youngsters, with the emphasis being on making a sustained contact with the ball through the impact area.

As with all golfers, once let loose on the course they should be allowed to go out and have some fun. Let them tee the ball up, hit as many shots as they like and not take a score. Above all, as a mum or dad don't push them too hard and don't become the expert analyst we have warned you about throughout this book!

LEFT
1. As long as you can turn your shoulders and lift your arms you have all the flexibility you will ever need.
2. Octogenarian Sir Christopher Lee, a school regular for more than forty years, still moves into the ball as dynamically as ever.
3. Learning the backswing hand line at an early age guarantees a lifetime's enjoyable golf.

77

There are many experts in golf (some even know what they are talking about) but you still can't listen to them

Along with the deluded amateur expert mentioned previously, we must warn you about a very different kind of expert. An expert who actually knows a great deal about the golf swing: The Tour Teacher.

We are not talking about the great many experienced and thoughtful coaches who have taught both professionals and amateurs and given a great deal of thought to how they approach instruction. We are referring to certain members of the younger generation. Those who were not good enough to make it on tour and as a career alternative turned to teaching to make themselves a name. We have done our time on tour and in no way wish to devalue their achievements in working with some of the finest players in the world. However, we must stress that their experience is limited to the swings

of the supremely talented. This type of Tour Teacher has very little first-hand knowledge of the problems encountered by the average golfer.

On numerous occasions some of our better-known pupils who have built strong swings through extensive tuition have fallen victim to the misplaced advice of The Tour Teacher. After spending some time building their swings in the school, they find themselves invited to a glitzy Pro-Am tournament and are privileged to play with some of the biggest names in golf. Almost without exception, their playing partners will compliment our pupils on their swings and fundamentals. They typically then offer a few tips of their own that could help them get even better. Often they suggest that the willing pupil should consult the pro's coaches, as a way of taking their game to the next level. And this is where it all begins to go so sadly wrong.

The Tour Teacher (and the tour player) know virtually nothing about the travails of the layman golfer

The Tour Teacher (and the tour player) know virtually nothing about the travails of the layman golfer. Slowly, but surely, the swings that we have so carefully constructed become contaminated through tinkering, and two or three years later – when the pupil's swing has deteriorated – we are left to pick up the pieces of what were once perfectly good golf swings.

In fairness, many of our pupils have improved other areas of their game after working with tour teachers, such as the ability to navigate their way around the course and their short game and mental approach. But the ability to drive the ball long and straight with consistency, the ability to find the greens easily with their irons – the real joy of golf – has been lost as they struggle halfway down either side of the fairway.

Before they even participate in these events we warn our pupils of the dangers of listening to pros and their coaches. But who can blame them? They have built their swings in a Knightsbridge basement from two old blokes and some antiquated video equipment. So when they are catapulted on to the world's finest golf courses to play with the world's greatest players and receive counsel from their coaches, they inevitably think that this is where the future of their swing lies.

The moral of the story is, if you have been having lessons with your local club pro and are happy with the progress you are making, don't tamper with his work. Don't think that consulting a big-name tour coach will fast-track you to the next level. Your pro knows your swing better than anyone. He may not have the latest gadgetry or write a column for a golf magazine, but his knowledge is far more valuable to you than that of the fledgling tour teacher, so stick with it.

78

Pupil's tale - Eve Branson

Having not taken golf seriously before, it was with some trepidation that at the age of seventy-two, on the instruction of my son Richard, I booked a lesson. I needn't have worried. My regular Tuesday lesson gave me my most precious half hour of the week. To my joy and utter delight, my golf improved immediately. Within a year, I was competing alongside some of the best players in Europe in a glitzy Monaco Pro-Am. I can't tell you how much I enjoy my golf and appreciate what the teachings of the Knightsbridge Golf School have done for me.

ABOVE
Eve Branson at the Monaco Pro-Am

79

A tale of two golfers
part two

It is another Tuesday morning and two beginners are being pushed and pulled through the basic swing shapes that have been taught at the School for the past sixty years.

In the far bay we have a slight, silver-haired lady in her early seventies who we shall call 'Lady V'. She goes through her pre-shot routine, fastens the Velcro on her left-hand glove and buttons her designer cardigan. As instructed, she draws the club back to the top of the backswing, pauses momentarily and delivers the clubhead firmly and squarely into the back of the ball. With a sharp crack it rockets forward, dissecting the centre of the net; the balance at the finish is pro-like, she drops her arms to hip height and checks the clubface. It is square. That's the fourth good shot in a row. Not bad considering that until her 72nd birthday she had never even held a golf club.

In the other bay stands Metalman: tattooed, clad in black and an assortment of body piercings. Twenty years ago, the last place you would expect to find his type would have been in a golf school. But that was then and this is now. Golf is his new stimulant. It's legal and he loves it. He embraces the game with an enthusiasm he hasn't felt since, as a twelve-year-old, he picked up his first guitar. This man has talent, and could become a very low handicap golfer. His golfing future is as bright as his 360 Modena is red.

Metalman hadn't planned on it, but the following week he finds himself at the golf range with two of his pals, Pete and Paul. His ideal first golf date would have been a gentle introduction with the elegant Lady V, but his friends had heard he was taking golf lessons and were keen to take him to the range for the bragging rights as to who has got the biggest one.

Pete is first to draw his weapon. It's got a long shaft, a big shiny head and feels good in his hands. He pulls it back, waves it around and with an almighty swipe crashes the ball into the wooden bay divider. The boys collapse in a fit of giggles whilst the rest of the range dives for cover. "You know your trouble? You are standing too near to the ball after you have hit it," quips Paul.

Next up is Paul, a man who considers himself something of an expert in golf technique. He has read every book under the sun and has just purchased a new DVD

Tips from the Tour by the new Goldenballs of golf instruction, Brett Devine.

As he takes his address, his head swims with yet another new set of golfing ideas and theories. So far, he has stood over the ball for fifty-two seconds. When he eventually does get the club moving, it is not a pretty sight and certainly not the sort of swing you expect to see from a man who now has the advantage of using *Tips from the Tour*. The movement is stiff, it's knotty and the result eminently forgettable. The ball takes off at knee height and comes to rest by the hundred yard marker.

Metalman is a little bemused. He had heard his pals were really keen golfers, heard them bragging about their huge drives and arguing over who has the biggest one. He really did expect a little more. Still – what does he know? Carefully prepared at the school, he hasn't even hit a ball in anger, let alone the open air. However, that is about to change. He selects a five iron, tees the ball up and draws the club back to the top of the backswing, pauses momentarily and delivers the clubhead firmly and squarely into the back of the ball.

It starts low and climbs swiftly as it pushes forwards through the air, landing seventy yards past Paul's strained effort. He hits four

LEFT
Hannah has only recently taken up golf. She has learnt and perfected the swing's crucial backswing hand line, although her knees may appear a little too bent here. Her future enjoyment is guaranteed. The only thing that could spoil it is if it is contaminated by some useless piece of advice from a self-styled expert. Beware! There are many experts in golf, and some are so good they even boast a handicap of 22.

more, five more, and the result is the same each time. His pals are gobsmacked.

Paul is not amused – this is war! He gets out his new £400 driver, hits three shots sideways, four along the ground, but then it happens – he catches one and boy does it fly, almost to the boundary fence at the back of the range. "Pick the bones out of that one," he boasts, and hands Metalman his driver. Unfortunately, our tattooed friend has never even held a driver before (that was due to be next week's lesson). Nevertheless he feels obliged to give it a try. It is a lot longer than he is used to. He had been promised a gentle progression from mid-iron to driver. He feels a little awkward, and struggles. His efforts simply can't match those of his iron and so it begins. It is the seminal moment, the moment this man's whole golfing future is turned on its head.

"You know what you are doing wrong, you're not creating enough resistance in your hips on the backswing, and you're moving your head, and your wrists should break more, and you should take it further back," says Paul. And so on, and so forth.

Over the next half hour our golfing new boy is given scores of tips and pieces of advice. Almost every theory and technique is resurrected in a veritable 'golfing masterclass'.

Metalman is totally confused. Slowly but surely, his carefully constructed golf swing is beginning to disintegrate. He can't hit the driver and eventually drops back to his five iron. But it is too late; it's gone. He has lost the feeling and can't find the middle of the blade. He leaves the range a little down-hearted and confused. Surely his friend knows what he is talking about? He has played for years, spent a small fortune on instruction material and has even got a handicap... 22 (whatever that means).

A month later, on England's south coast, a very different tale is unfolding. Lady V has been to the range a couple of times and is now enjoying her first experience of the golf course. She is going along very nicely indeed. In fact, she hasn't missed a shot all morning. OK, she is not playing out of bunkers. She is not even playing from the rough, she has been told not to. She is simply concentrating on making a nice crisp contact with the ball: get it airborne and get it moving. Lady V is alone. She never did hear from Metalman and hasn't seen him at the school for ages. She has had offers from friends but has decided she would be better off alone. Even before her first outdoor outing, alarm bells were ringing. It seemed to her that there really *are* an extraordinary number of experts in golf. Whenever she mentioned to anyone that she was taking up golf, they all came back to her with advice on what clubs to buy, where to play and how to swing a club. One of her friends has even recommended a marvellous new book by a mysterious 'Doctor Z', a nuclear physicist who has turned his scientific expertise to the golf swing and has come up with some interesting new theories and techniques. Doctor Z's book may be a wonderful publication, but Lady V doesn't want anything to confuse her.

She is quite happy to learn one method, one model and to stick with it. She can relate to this approach.

As a young woman she first learnt to ride at a long-established stables from a very tough task master. In an effort to improve her technique she had read an article by some dashing Argentinean polo players and was keen to incorporate some of their flair into her style.

Learn the basics: one model, one method – and stick to it!

Unfortunately, this upset her balance so much that she ended up falling off the horse and breaking her left wrist and right leg.

Her instructor had no sympathy with her and told her it served her right for interfering with her instruction.

Lady V never did see Metalman in the school again, but a year later their paths did cross, when she was invited to a glamorous Pro-Am tournament in the Caribbean. She first spotted Metalman on the practice ground surrounded by his new friends, the young lions of the professional tour. She also noticed an exotic oriental man monotonously repeating the mantra "BE POSITIVE, THINK POSITIVE; BE POSITIVE, THINK POSITIVE". And she was aware of a rather painful looking contraption that Metalman had connected to his right wrist, left elbow and right shoulder. Lady V found his swing unrecognisable. As fate would have it, they were drawn to play together and she was a little concerned. She would be out of her depth; after all he had his battery of golf instructors, a mind guru and his swing contraptions. All she had was her structured swing shape.

Metalman hit some great golf shots. He hit the ball a good distance and had three or four dead straight drives. However, he also hit three a hundred yards right, three even further left and the rest into the Caribbean Sea!

Lady V's round was far less adventurous; she hit fourteen down the middle, three to the right hand rough and she pulled one left. Taking her 24 handicap into account, she finished with a net 68, long after Metalman had stopped counting.

Both tales are based on true stories. Only the names have been changed to protect the guilty. The moral should be self-evident. Learn a swing model – and stick to it. There will always be experts who are only too willing to offer advice; there will always be this or that latest discovery; tour professionals will always offer tips, often good ones, but, if taken out of context, very damning. There is nothing unorthodox or controversial about our swing model. Any club pro should be able to check your positions and the basic swing fundamentals. In conclusion we offer one bit of advice: find yourself a good club professional and stick with him!

80

Sir Christopher Lee

Over the years many of the great and the good have descended the stairs to our basement studio to learn the secrets of our modelled swing. Sir Christopher Lee has been a school regular longer than we have. He first took lessons in the mid-sixties and has been coming in for his regular 'check-ups' ever since.

A first class golfer with a low single figure handicap, Christopher has had the privilege of playing with some of the greatest players of the last sixty years – Hogan, Nicklaus, Player, Palmer, Ballesteros, Faldo and more. The list is endless and he has entertained us over the last thirty years with stories of his time with the golfing greats. In fact, as interesting as we find these stories, we sometimes have

to stop him in full flow. We've looked at the clock and twenty minutes of the thirty-minute lesson have gone!

Sir Christopher Lee is one of the few stars who has the same physical presence in real life as he has on the cinema screen. He is huge, has classic good looks and piercing eyes. However, there really is nothing remotely sinister about Christopher. He is absolutely charming. As mentioned earlier, he is still a regular of ours and, at eighty-eight, can still regularly score well under his age. He makes as many films as ever and is a hero to a new generation for his roles in *Lord of the Rings* and *Star Wars*, and is also performing on heavy metal albums and appearing at their concerts!

81

Technology is all very well but…

We don't use computers and we don't use simulators. Not that we have got anything against them. It is simply that we don't have the time to use them, as we are too busy pushing pupils through the essential swing shapes. If we spent twenty minutes staring at a screen we would have no time left for the practical. It is all very well for a student to understand what he is doing badly and see it illustrated by the latest hi-tech equipment, but unless he has a method to execute the corrections to the swing, the lesson is worthless.

Simulators are good fun and centres such as the marvellous Urban Golf provide brilliant entertainment. However, they do nothing to improve your golf swing.

Everyone hates seeing themselves on screen and one student of ours told her husband that she wouldn't come in again until she lost some weight! Even Bryan Ferry, the 'King of Cool', was horrified when he first saw himself on our video screen. "Who's that?" he said. "It's you," we answered. "Oh my God!" he replied and we thought, "If he thinks he looks bad then what hope is there for the rest of us?" Thankfully our lady client eventually returned and is happy with her new figure, though not as happy as she is with her elegant new swing.

82

The greatest game ever played

In the summer of 2004, three new visitors to the school made us feel that our story had turned a full circle. *The Greatest Game Ever Played* was written by Mark Frost and told the story of the 1913 US Open. It focused on how Francis Ouimet, a nineteen-year-old American amateur, defeated Harry Vardon and Ted Ray, the superstar British golfers of their day, who had been sent over to America by newspaper baron Lord Northcliffe to reclaim the US Open from the upstart Americans (who had won the trophy in 1912).

The book received great reviews and Disney bought the film rights. Mark Frost had heard great things about the school and had no hesitation in sending Stephen Marcus (Ted Ray), Stephen Dillane (Harry Vardon) and George Asprey (Wilfred Reid) to replicate the swings and the mannerisms of these three great British golfers. We were more than familiar with these swings, as Leslie King originally built his swing model on the actions of Ted Ray and Harry Vardon.

Just over a year later, we were invited to a private viewing and watched the swings of Vardon and Ray come alive again on the cinema at Disney's offices. We were speechless at seeing our names rolling down the screens in the credits of a major Hollywood production!

LEFT
Stephen Dillane (Harry Vardon), George Asprey (Wilfred Reid) and Stephen Marcus (Ted Ray), in a signed still from the movie.

83

Lord Lucan

Along with the great and the good, the School has also taught those that may be described as from the darker side. The mysterious Lord Lucan was a regular pupil of Leslie King's and was at the School the very day before infamously disappearing following the murder of his children's nanny. The police interviewed Leslie King during the course of their enquiries and typically he told them that he was not prepared to discuss his clients with anyone. Some years later he was quoted in a book about Lord Lucan stating that, out of all the members of the aristocracy he has taught, none had stronger hands than 'Lucky Lucan'. Interestingly, some thirty-five years later, a set of clubs that Lord Lucan bought for his wife still sits in our office, together with six Dunlop 65s, still in their original wrappers.

84

No match for the maharajah

Ask us about Leslie King and we'll tell you that he never turned anybody away. He never told anybody they weren't good enough, for the simple reason that he was convinced he could help anybody, however badly coordinated, inflexible or dyslexic, to play the game to an enjoyable standard.

Every rule, though, must have its exception. The exception in this case arrived at the school one day in the shape of an Indian maharajah, resplendent in traditional robes, turban and a ceremonial sword. There was even a manservant in attendance.

Mr King suggested the prince approach the mat and take a few swings, and stood opposite him to observe. The maharajah duly set up the ball, produced a half-decent backswing and then suddenly swung the club back, baseball-style, at head height. Mr King ducked just in time as the club whistled over his head. Apparently unruffled, Mr King suggested the prince have another go. "You see this mat?" he said, bashing the mat two or three times with a golf club. "Just hit this mat." Again, Mr King was forced to duck, just as he was on the third attempt. And, with that, Mr King stepped forward, prised the club from the maharajah's fingers and said in a gentle yet firm voice: "Sir, you must never, ever play golf."

As far as we know, he never did, which is probably fortunate for his prospective playing partners as well as his manservant. We still maintain, as Mr King did, that everyone is capable of playing golf. With, of course, the odd, resplendent exception.

Des Lynam

Des Lynam's first words to our rather amateurish answerphone greeting were "it seems you need as much help with your answerphone as I do with my golf swing!" Des enjoyed our lessons and was convinced that we could create an interesting and exciting TV golf instruction series ("interesting" and "exciting" — words not usually associated with golf instruction!). Des presented his ideas to the BBC and together we made a small TV promo. Unfortunately nothing came of that project but we'd like to put on record that Des gave his time and efforts for nothing more than his goodwill to us. We hope he remains a good friend of the School for many years to come.

85

Pitching

The short game is now a highly specialised area of instruction. Scores of books have been written, DVDs produced and a wealth of material is now available to all. Much can be learnt from these teachings, but this wisdom will prove of little value if a player has failed to master the crucial backswing hand line.

Without question, the reason why the majority of golfers struggle with their short game is that they twist or roll the club during the takeaway to hip height stage of the backswing. This, combined with the destructive influence of the subconscious reflex, is the reason why the topped, fluffed or shanked approach shot is endemic in so many golfers.

To pitch and chip correctly is essential to good golf. Hitting the ball over 260 yards and peppering the pin with the irons is great fun. But if your short game is poor you will always be as average as your scorecard suggests.

As dogmatic as we are in our teaching, we would have no hesitation in sending a pupil to a short game specialist providing, of course, that the backswing's hand line had been fully mastered and committed to muscle memory.

If your hand line is sound, you should treat the standard pitch shot as no more than a half swing played from a square stance. But if you feel that it helps you, open the stance slightly by drawing the left foot back. Swing the club back to hip height on the backswing and follow through to hip height at the finish.

When playing full pitch shots, it is important to pay close attention to the follow through at the completion of the swing. The shaft should be vertical, almost in line with the pin. If the shaft is allowed to go to the horizontal, it is a sure sign that you have used too much wrist action through the ball.

If you finish with the shaft vertical you will find that your pitch shots land a lot nearer to the pin, due to the greater control achieved by the hands staying together through impact and beyond. With this in mind, it is important to mention that even the playing of a half shot requires a certain amount of firmness. Don't allow yourself to quit on the shot simply because the ball has a short way to travel. Tentative approach shots rarely work.

Pitching sequences

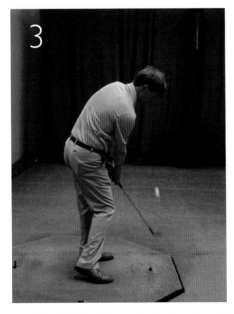

1–4. The pitch shot is merely a 'half version' of the full swing.

A, B. When playing full pitch shots the backswing must be complete and the shaft at the finish should be vertical.

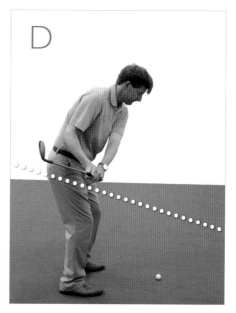

C. The backswing hand line sequence has taught you that, ideally, as a slight exaggeration, the shaft must run on the line of the bicep. However, it is perfectly acceptable for the shaft to run on the line of the right arm.
D. Once the shaft has been allowed to drop below the line of the right arm the action is destroyed.

86

The bunker shot

The bunker shot, the explosion from a well-kept trap with the adequate amount of fine dry sand, is the simplest, most effortless stroke in the game. As you address the ball, you should slightly open the clubface and put your feet fairly close together. Plant the feet into the sand and concentrate on the sand one or two inches behind the ball. On the downswing, the clubhead is going to contact this spot in the sand – not the ball (as in every other shot you play).

Swing the club back slowly and smoothly, slightly outside the line. As you come down, the clubhead will come through the sand, so the ball is collected on a cushion of sand which carries it clear as it pops, lifelessly, onto the green. When playing this shot, be careful that you don't shorten the backswing or the follow through. The swing should be full and free-flowing.

If the sand is wet or crusty, you will have to take the ball out cleanly or even skid it out. We advise you to learn these shots in the bunker under personal supervision. They are extremely precise and are best dealt with on an individual basis.

First master the standard bunker stroke. So simple yet so effective.

RIGHT
A cushion of sand carries the ball clear and pops it lifelessly onto the green.

87

Chipping

It is no surprise to say that the chip is equally affected by the rolling, twisting action that ruins the majority of swings. In the chipping action the wrist must again hinge gently on the backswing whilst keeping the clubhead to the right of the hands. The club must then move through the ball in unison with the body. If the body is static, the hands and arms lose control.

Chipping sequence

1. The clubhead stays to the right of the hands on the backswing

2. The clubhead remains to the right of the hands in the follow through.

88

The topped, fluffed or shanked approach shot and the miserable yipped putt

It is not only the tee and iron shot that is susceptible to the reflex. Its curse runs right down to the pitch, chip, bunker shot and putt. The player with a consistent short game action and tempo can ruin his card by subconsciously pushing the club forwards or steering his shot towards the green.

The bunker shot is equally affected. Although a player may trust his swing, a reflex urge to dig the ball out of the sand can frequently leave him languishing in the trap.

With this in mind it is no surprise to see how, when faced with a tricky putt, a player's action can desert him as the same reflex flares up and forces him to prod or steer the ball into the expectant cup. A good putter's action should be similar to that of a snooker player, where a smooth, even-paced movement must be executed away from, to and through the static ball.

RIGHT
It can happen to the best of us.

89

Putting

It is often said that the man who can pitch and putt is a match for anyone. This is true only to the extent that a pitch and one putt means a stroke saved. But the man who is more than a match for most is he who can hit accurate second shots to the heart of the green, provided he can also putt. This man is faced with the welcome prospect not of saving a stroke against par, but of gaining one by rolling down the putt for a birdie. The top player must pick up more strokes than he saves. To do this he must putt well to take advantage of the opportunities he has set up for himself.

The finest aid to putting is confidence, which is gained mainly from walking up and picking the ball out of the hole! In putting, nothing succeeds like success. Confidence is also gained from the feeling that you are going to strike the ball as it should be struck. Several factors combine to achieve this end.

First, the putter must be lined up square to the line of the putt. Then it must be taken along that line and kept square to the line. It must be returned to the ball and into the brief follow through, still on that line and still square. The movement of the putter blade should be economical either side of the ball and be of the shallowest of arcs, resembling a slide rule action.

Good putters display a variety of methods in managing the behaviour of the putter blade, as putting is very much an individual science. Indifferent or bad putters show an equally wide variety of less successful ideas.

However, practically all the really good ones conform to certain common fundamentals. The stance is balanced and comfortable and tension is not allowed to creep in at any stage of the stroke. The eyes are directly over the ball and the hands grip the club as lightly as possible, no tighter than is necessary for control of the putter. The back of the left hand and the palm of the right are square and the palm of the right is square, to the line of the putt. Both thumbs are on top of the shaft.

The reverse overlap grip is the most popular, overlapping the forefinger of the left hand across the fingers of the right. However, many fine putters use the normal overlap, while others use the two-handed or reverse-handed grip. All have proved successful and it is up to the individual to discover which is best for him.

The backswing should be kept slow and the head and body maintained perfectly still throughout the stroke. Addressing the ball with a slight knock-kneed feeling will help greatly in keeping the body motionless throughout the stroke.

During his playing career, golf's best ever commentator Peter Alliss missed more than a few big prizes by lapsing on the three and

four footers. He had a tendency to take the blade back too quickly on these short putts. A great putter will keep the blade low both back and through the ball and the face of the club square all the way through to its final position. Most putting problems we encounter are caused by the clubhead turning in or being flicked through the ball.

A great practice drill to promote the correct hand movement is to cut a piece of sellotape 6–7 inches long and place it on your carpet. Place a ball on one end. Now, taking your putter, simply play the ball, stopping at the other end with the tape in the middle of the putter blade and the blade square. This ensures there is no break of the left wrist as the hands move through the ball.

As you practise this drill, try to remember that you should concentrate on hitting it accurately along the first six inches of its path. Get the line and note a spot six inches ahead of the ball, along that line. Then make certain of striking the ball so it passes over that spot. The simple theory is that the player can do no more. After that first six inches providence takes over!

One final note on putting practice. It is one thing to knock the ball into the hole on the practice green and quite a different matter doing likewise under pressure out on the course. It is on the practice green that you work on your method and acquire the initial confidence from striking the ball effectively with the putter blade.

Practise putts of all lengths, but give your main attention to those from ten feet down. Don't play a succession of

balls from the same spot. Vary the line by moving round the hole.

Before you go out on a serious round of golf, practise a few 'tap-ins', take your time and putt the ball into the hole from two feet to eighteen inches or even less. Eighteen inches or less? Certainly if you laugh this off now, you will soon be changing your attitude when you have missed one or two tiddlers with a card and pencil in your pocket. One of our pupils could have been a very fine golfer indeed if he was more confident with his putter.

This player has putting inconsistencies which throw a considerable strain on his play through the green. He has confessed to us that when he first started playing he only played golf with his friends and they always gave each other the twelve-to-eighteen inch putts. However, when he joined a golf club and started playing in competitions, he realised he had to knock the ball in from twelve to eighteen inches and had never really done it before. When asked to, he got scared, thought he would miss it – and did! Similar short putts are being missed by golfers every day. They must not be regarded as a mere formality. Practise these and be sure you are slow back from the ball, deliberate on the return movement and that you make a point of seeing the right forearm past the spot where the ball lay. This is very important. It keeps the putter blade square and on line through the ball and stops you looking up too soon.

90

Creating an end product

By now you should know what we mean by creating a swing model and how paranoid we are about maintaining its purity. To give you a further idea of its meaning we will now aim to relate it to something very different, but in some ways just the same.

If an artist were to create a sculpture of the human body, he would have a defined idea of its completed image before his work had begun. The sculptor would work from raw materials and sculpt each limb in proportion to the next, blending it into the torso to create perfect proportion and total symmetry.

This is similar to what we do when we build our golf swings. We create an overall structure and blend each swing position into the next. Just like the sculptor, we know exactly how the end product will look and how the swing will perform before the pupil has even gripped the club.

Imagine how our sculptor would feel if, just before his work was complete, four or five artists began to chip away at his masterpiece. Changing the shape of the nose, shortening a finger here or there, moving a leg etc. The sculptor would be distraught to see that what he had so lovingly planned and created had been destroyed. It would end up looking a frightful mess. This is exactly how we feel when the swings we have so carefully constructed have been destroyed by others adding tips and bits of advice to different areas of a crafted swing. The whole structure falls apart.

We always warn our charges in advance of what will happen when they are released into the golfing world. We tell them that from their first bucket of driving range balls advice will be forthcoming from well-meaning souls, but we implore them not to listen. They assure us that they are good pupils and will not listen to anyone, but invariably they soon do. To us it is like bringing up your children the right way and warning them of the dangers that lie in wait in the outside world. You can warn them repeatedly, but once they are on their own temptation is hard to resist.

It is always sad to see a pupil with a promising swing lose, perhaps forever, the chance to be very good at this very frustrating game.

Stick with your club pro, follow your own path as you teach yourself through this book, back your judgement on your own development despite any flattering or disheartening pointers to the contrary. No one knows your swing better than yourself and your teacher.

Mr King gave similar advice to his young professional protégés some time ago. At the time we thought he was mad. Surely the willing pupil can learn something from taking on different pieces of advice? Over time experience has shown us that the Old Master knew exactly what he was talking about and each day we despair as we realise we are turning into that curmudgeonly, yet charming, old man.

91

Girl power

For many years the image of women's golf was, quite frankly, appalling. Blue rinses, tweed skirts and threadbare cardigans were truly the order of the day. Thankfully, and at long last, that image is most certainly changing as more glamorous girls and high-profile celebrities are now taking up the game.

Jodie Kidd and Catherine Zeta-Jones are two of the most recognised and keenest golfers of this generation and a few years ago we had the pleasure of teaching former Spice Girl Geri Halliwell. Geri was recommended to us by a close friend. She seemed to enjoy her lessons and showed great enthusiasm and good aptitude. We are unsure if she ever took up the game seriously but her interest proves that times are certainly changing. Incidentally she was always accompanied by her great pal Harry the Shih Tzu, who obediently observed from the safety of her designer handbag.

Talking of designers, it's great to see that major fashion houses are now designing clothes and accessories specifically for the lady golfers. When we take our female pupils to the course for the first time, often the first place they want to see is the pro shop to engage in a little retail therapy!

Technique-wise, the female golfer is no different from the male. However, for the lady it is crucial that their swing model is tuned to absolute perfection. Due to a man's build, with the momentum they generate through impact they can, to a certain extent, get away with a few individual mannerisms. For golfers with less upper body strength, this is not the case and their technique must be that much better and purer. We think this is why women make such good pupils – they're aware of their physical limitations and work meticulously on refining their technique.

Thankfully the attitude of some Golf Clubs to lady golfers is now also changing. For years the lady member was seen as a bit of a nuisance and sometimes membership was actively discouraged. One legendary sign at an extremely prestigious club announced, and this is absolutely true: 'NO WOMEN OR DOGS ALLOWED.'

We are pleased to report that this pronouncement has now been removed!

92

Ant and Dec's All Star Cup

In August 2005 we were pleased be to be part of the All Star Cup, a Ryder Cup-style contest between celebrity golfers from Europe and the United States. The All Star Cup was the brainchild of TV's Ant and Dec, who had taken a few lessons with us the previous winter.

The contest took place at Celtic Manor, the venue for the 2010 Ryder Cup, over the Bank Holiday weekend and proved to be a big success, with an attendance of over 25,000 – a respectable figure for many a major golf tournament.

It was also a triumph in that it brought many newcomers to the game. They were inspired by the glamour, the setting and the realisation that golf was finally losing its stuffy, fuddy-duddy image. The United States team featured – amongst others – Mark Spitz, Cheryl Ladd and Kenny G, and was captained by Michael Douglas whilst his wife, Catherine Zeta Jones, represented Europe along with the likes of Ronan Keating, Chris Evans and former footballer Ian Wright.

Unfortunately, despite access to allegedly the world's finest coaches, barely one of them could swing the club correctly through golf's master key, the takeaway to hip height hand line. They all twisted the club into the backswing and were almost identical!

One handicapper, Kenny G, was well aware of his takeaway problems and was working hard on correcting it. Meanwhile, most of the others just flashed the club back and through in the hope of hitting it. In all fairness, they hit lots of great shots, but equally there were some truly horrendous shots. This is the problem with seriously flawed fundamentals – there is always a disaster lurking around the corner. These players can be going along very nicely and then it starts: they snap hook a shot, they shank a shot, fluff a shot, top a shot – take your pick.

Some of these mid-handicap celebrities have the talent to go all the way to single figures if only someone would get hold of them and build them a sound modelled swing. We haven't seen Ant and Dec for some time now, but hope that one day we can do for them what we have done for tens of thousands of others over the years.

93
The Dunhill Links Challenge

Over the last few years we have been regular visitors to Scotland's Dunhill Links Challenge. Played at St Andrews, Carnoustie and Kingsbarns, the Dunhill is a premier European tour event that doubles up as a Pro-Am tournament. Celebrities, sportsmen and some seriously high-flying businessmen from all over the world compete.

It is a great event and, being played in October, has the feel of a European tour end-of-term bash, with competitors and visitors enjoying wonderful Scottish hospitality and the many fine watering holes located around the St Andrews Bay area.

It was where Hugh Grant first emerged as a keen golfer after spending the summer of 2001 learning a modelled swing with us in Knightsbridge. Hugh had been a part-time pupil long before he became a household name. He never really played much golf in those days but in early 2000 purchased a series of lessons for his father who was keen to spend his retirement years on the golf course.

His dad's enthusiasm rubbed off on Hugh and the following year he took up a game that, we heard, he was somewhat reluctant to embrace. From his first visit it was obvious that he had been a former pupil. He used a short-ish controlled backswing and moved through the ball into a balanced, poised finish. He was a good example of our early

teaching when the school's standard was to teach the finish first. A wonderful way to learn how to play golf.

An hour into Hugh's Pro-Am debut the school's answerphone began to fill with messages from pupils who were watching him accompany Sam Torrance as they quickly made their way up the leaderboard. They told us that Hugh was playing faultless golf and Sky's commentators were heaping praise on what they believed was one of the best amateur swings they had seen in years. True to form, when interviewed, Hugh thanked the Knightsbridge Golf School for all our hard work.

Watching the highlights that evening took us back some twenty-five years to when we were teaching 1960s pop icon and star of *Budgie*, Adam Faith. Adam signed up at the school whilst recovering from crashing first his car and then his helicopter! He concluded that golf was perhaps a safer pastime and the golf course a perfect place to rehabilitate. He was a good pupil and made swift progress. Within no time he was contacted by the BBC who wanted him to compete in the hugely popular *Pro Celebrity Golf* series.

Our good friend and erstwhile colleague Eddie Cogle accompanied him up to Gleneagles and he played some marvellous golf. His professional partners were amazed at the quality of his swing and told

The Dunhill Links Challenge 2007.

viewers that his technique was as pure as any they'd seen. Like Hugh, Adam was a gentleman and was so grateful to Leslie King that he consistently thanked him throughout the entire transmission, much to the amusement of the show's host, and a true hero of ours, Peter Alliss! His professional partners Tom Weiskopf and Peter Oosterhuis were amazed.

Hugh continued to perform throughout his week at the Dunhill and made it all the way to the final day of competition. Highly commendable for a player who had spent most of his golfing life hitting balls into the back of a net.

Many of our school's regulars are also Dunhill regulars and for one of our good friends it's almost the only golf he gets to play all year. We cannot name him, as he hasn't even got a handicap, and to play in the event the strictest of rules states that a competitor must have a maximum official handicap of 18! So you can imagine our trepidation when on his first outing he took his place on the first tee. We closed our eyes and waited for the sound of the ball hitting the tee box. We needn't have worried – he struck his drive to a distance of almost three hundred yards! However the tee box did receive a direct hit from its next occupant, a single figure golfer and captain of one of the country's most prestigious golf clubs. His nerves obviously got the better of him, unlike our protégé who stood up, made the most simple of modelled swings and accepted the applause of the assembled gallery!

94

The mind

Golf is a game that will always attack your nerves and exploit your imagination if you allow it to. Various estimates as to the extent to which golf is 'mental' as distinct from purely 'physical' have been expounded in both locker-rooms and in print. Some pundits, both amateur and professional, have even maintained that golf is as much as 75% mental.

We believe it's impossible to venture an accurate, or worthwhile, opinion on the matter as it naturally varies according to the make-up and outlook of the individual. But one thing we are convinced of: no game throws out a stronger challenge to the temperament of the player. Some face this challenge and beat it, but others never come to master their emotions and, consequently, never achieve all of which they are capable.

James may have a fine method but suspect temperament. Jack may be ideally equipped temperamentally, but his technique will show obvious flaws. Both James and Jack will meet with a certain degree of success, but neither will attain the standard which could have been his if he had overcome his weakness of temperament in the case of James, or of technique in the case of Jack.

The instructor, like the doctor, can only prescribe so far. Just as the doctor must have the cooperation and the will to get well of his patient, so the golf instructor requires perseverance and determined effort on the part of the pupil. The golf teacher can do his best for his pupil by helping him to acquire a sound and lasting method, making sure he understands what he is trying to do – and why.

The top players put their trust in their swing, particularly the great ones. It is true that when their swing is not working at its best, they have to buckle down to scrambling their figures. But no one knows better than they do themselves that they cannot 'scramble' indefinitely. Maybe they will get by for one round or part of round in a seventy-two hole tournament, but they must get it working smoothly without delay if they are to stay in the race.

As we write this, we are reminded of a story Mr King told us about a man who was placed under his hands for a mere half an hour in the late 1950s. What happened in this remarkable golfing episode not only clearly confirmed the effectiveness of his teaching method, it also demonstrated what can be accomplished out on the course, when the imagination and the mental process are under control.

The control, in this case, was exercised from outside. It was an experiment in post-hypnotic suggestion aimed at discovering how a player would perform when their mental doubts, fears and anxieties were divorced from the physical side of the game, by specially undertaken measures.

His pupil was a man, once a 3 handicap golfer, whose game had deteriorated over a period of years through lack of time and the demands of other interests.

An earlier experiment, when he had submitted to post-hypnotic suggestion, had proved inconclusive because of serious flaws in the physical side of his game. That is, of course, the way he swung the club. Leslie King's task, in the space of one thirty-minute lesson, was to reshape his swing and give him a delivery. He was able to do this, notwithstanding the limited time available, and before he left, the pupil was hitting well-struck shots into the net with the instruction and the confidence it had produced fresh in his mind.

Mr King had no further part in the experiment but learned later what happened when the pupil played his next round of golf the following day. The subject was told by the hypnotist that he would have no difficulty in remembering what Mr King had told him and what it felt like when he was swinging the club in the way in which he had been taught. He would be able to do exactly what he'd been told for the first nine holes and the last five. For four holes midway through the round, the 10th to the 13th inclusive, the remembering would be left entirely to him. In other words, his mind would be released from hypnotic control.

The following day he hit his full shots for the opening nine holes well-nigh to perfection. Note that in that half-hour lesson, Mr King had only had time to deal with the long game and when he was on the course next day his short approaches and his putting let him down at times.

He then came to the four 'de-controlled' holes where his game collapsed entirely. But with the last five holes to play – those five holes which the hypnotist had told him he would play well, he struck the ball straight and far, reaching each green in the regulation number of strokes.

We have related this story to underline the results to be obtained by relying implicitly on the swing, once you have given it the essential shape and fitted a delivery to it. We are not suggesting for one moment that aspiring golfers should reach for the telephone and call up the nearest hypnotist. Let's not take golf into a bizarre world where one man will contrive to beat another by three up and two to play, purely because he is

> Your refuge, when you feel the tension mounting, is the picture of the shape of your swing

the better subject of the two for post-hypnotic suggestion!

The experiment was undertaken purely to show how much more simple it would be to learn and progress if imagination and fear could be kept firmly under control. It clearly succeeded. It confirmed to Mr King what he already knew from his years of teaching experience – that no one can do better than their swing and delivery allow. Too many, too often cramp and distort the swing by letting their imaginations run wild.

There have been many occasions when we have dealt with pupils who have been too perfectionist for their own good. With good fundamentals, we have done much to improve these players' golf. But getting through to the perfectionist's mind is quite another thing. The bad shot must be accepted, shrugged off and forgotten. If this group of players could only discipline themselves to accept this philosophy, they could go far. Unfortunately, no matter how well they may be playing, as soon as they hit a bad shot, maybe well struck but nonetheless one which missed the target, they start to worry – the worst thing any golfer can do.

In match play the worrier allows a sharp thrust or a lucky break by an opponent to break his concentration and, in those circumstances, can never give undivided attention to his own game.

The bad and indifferent shots, the unexpected bursts of a match play opponent are bound to come in the course of a round. Your reflexes will inevitably play tricks now and again. Never forget that the hole you have just played is done with, and another hole with a fresh challenge awaits you on the next tee. Meet it in the right frame of mind, or you'll drop another stroke – perhaps more.

What we want to put across to you is that no man, however gifted a striker of the ball, is a machine. Mr King told us that the nearest he had seen come to it was Henry Cotton in his peak years, between 1935–37. His unscaleable height of play through the greens was as good as any human could hope for. Maybe Ben Hogan came close to it, but we have never seen anything like it in our lifetime.

Your refuge, when the imagination threatens to overcome self-discipline and when you feel the tension mounting, is the picture of the shape of your swing, which you should keep stored in your mind. Only through this mental picture can you feel and sense the position of the clubhead at the various stages of the movement.

Go on to the first tee at any golf club on a Sunday morning – what will you see? A weird conglomeration of styles: the snatcher, the floppy wristed chap who fans the ball, the player, as tense as a petrified rabbit waiting for the stoat to strike, and of course 'the bell ringer'. This is the player on the back foot at the finish of the swing, pulling his hands up and down like the man on duty at the Belfry.

We have seen many struggling players' swing black out right from the start. They roll it round their body, dropping the shaft on the back of the neck, at the top of the backswing. We remember Mr King remarking that so-and-so only needed to insert a razor blade into the club shaft to decapitate himself!

It does not require a golf student of any great knowledge or experience to sort out the Sunday morning rabbits from the Tigers. The former far outnumber the latter. Too many of these players lack a shaped swing. They have no mental picture of their intention other than a burning desire to thrash or steer the ball down the first fairway. They build up tension in mind and muscle even before they launch themselves into the backswing.

If you have a clear idea of your intention through a mental picture of a shaped swing, you can then concentrate on re-etching that picture without being plagued by doubts and fears about what is going to happen when the ball leaves the tee peg. You can do no more than apply your swing and allow it to do all that it can for you. What it is not capable of doing, you

cannot make by other measures. No golfer is better than his swing combined with his delivery.

The swing shape is the primary consideration. It will take you some way along the road. Then the quality of the delivery defines your limitations.

There are lots of golfers, professionals and amateurs in the low handicap ranks, striving to break through in tournaments. Many of them are what we call fifteen, or sixteen-hole, golfers. This is because they cannot keep their delivery going long enough to take them through a whole round of golf under pressure. It is not quite good enough for the job and – sooner or later – it lets them down.

You must put your swing and delivery to the sustained test of regular competition golf, if real headway is to be made. Only by absorbing the atmosphere and reducing the tension through regular experience of competitive play can you give your swing and delivery a real chance to make the grade.

Take your time moving round the course and settling yourself for the shot you are about to play. This doesn't mean strolling from one shot to another and then fussing and fiddling about before playing the ball. That is liable to do more harm than good.

You must attack and keep on attacking. A cricketer can make fifty runs and those fifty

(The bad shot
must be accepted,
shrugged off and
forgotten)

runs will remain against his name, whatever rash act he may commit in the next over. How different with the golfer. He may be two or three under fours for fifteen holes and wreck his card by blowing up over the next three. He cannot rest on what he has achieved. He must go on adding good golf to the good golf he has already played. He can best do this by keeping on the attack. Playing safe only leads to tentative golf and before he knows it, he is quitting on the shot and cutting his swing off before it has entered the apex.

By attacking we don't mean that you should crash your way around the course with a swashbuckling disregard for the risks entailed. Maintain discretion, your temper and your smoothness of swing at all times. You are not withdrawing from the attack into a defensive frame of mind when you take an iron from the tee where a cross hazard is likely to gobble up a well-struck shot with the driver. Taking an iron when presented with such a situation is not playing safe. It is planning your assault on the hole, showing sound sense in club selection and course management. The attacking spirit must be blended with the ability to make a calm assessment of each problem as it arises.

Never give up hope and allow your game to slacken after a bad hole or a run of slipped shots has led you to the premature belief that your chance of winning or finishing well up the field has disappeared. You do not know how the remainder of the competitors are faring or that your fortunes are not going to take a sudden turn for the better. And the winning score may well prove to be higher than you estimate. You don't need to post the best score ever, just better than that of your opponents.

In match-play sharp changes of fortune are common. You may find yourself several holes down. But if you seize the chance when it comes, it may well turn out to be the start of recovery and the player whose lead is being eaten away is under greater pressure than his opponent who is fast making up leeway. Always keep in mind that you are not beaten, neither have you won, until the final putt drops into the hole.

Make up your mind to go on playing each stroke as it comes, giving your undivided attention to that particular stroke regardless of what may have happened before or problems which may or may not lie ahead. In this way you will learn with experience the invaluable, yet elusive, art of stringing your shots together – one of the subtle virtues in which great players excel.

Finally, we are asked what the player should think of when playing the shot. Now it should not be necessary for us to remind you that you cannot have a series of 'dos and don'ts' running backwards and forwards in your mind as you address the ball and move into your swing. This is your surest way to wreck your hopes of a good shot even before you start. Many experienced players declare that they think of one feature of the operation and no more. We go along with them – up to a point.

For example, if you develop a tendency to hasten the movement from the top of the swing, you can make sure that you smooth out the movement back to the ball by taking care to start the downswing with a slow, easy swing, with the hands and arms.

However, please heed this warning. Over-concentration on any one stage of the swing may lead to exaggeration with a consequent distortion of the swing as a whole. We are aiming at a smooth balanced movement all the way and must maintain that when a flaw has been eradicated. You must place your entire trust in the mental picture of the shaped swing and the delivery you have built into it. The more you can discipline yourself to do this, and keep doing it in spite of all distractions and changing circumstances, the more natural it will become, both physically and mentally. The intention is formed in the mind. The muscles must be trained to obey, not to take charge.

In summary, your swing and the delivery you have fitted into it will do all that can possibly be done to give your peak performance.

95

Practice makes perfect – or does it?

Gary Player, a former pupil of Leslie King, once famously said, "The more I practise, the luckier I get." A fine statement and often used to endorse the strong work ethic of those at the very top of their chosen profession. However, it is important to realise that, in golf, practice can only make perfect if you are working on perfecting a structured swing model that creates the hand line of the naturally gifted golfer.

To practise without structure is simply a waste of time. To bash and thrash a bucket of balls all over the practice ground or driving range will only ever succeed in perfecting your faults.

By now you will be well aware of this, but even if you are working correctly on building a swing, you should still take care whilst practising and ensure that you practise in a way that most helps in nurturing your new swing.

The good news is that some of your best practice can be done without even leaving the home or office. Simply by moving through the swing's positions and drills you will gradually cement the feeling of your new swing positions. Using a mirror is, of course, a must, as you can see exactly where you are at each and every stage of the swing. It worked for Telly Savalas (page 60).

Pupils often express surprise and disbelief when, after their first lesson, we tell them not to practise. This goes against everything they have ever been told but the reason is quite simple – after one lesson the pupil simply doesn't know the feeling of the swing movements well enough and any attempt to practise them would be fruitless. Over the next few lessons we push and pull them through the same movements and as they begin to make the shapes themselves, they are free to practise as much as they wish.

When you feel confident enough to take your swing to the range or practice ground, try to select a central position or driving range bay; never hit your shots diagonally from the right side over to the left. Play along a defined line to a defined target. Hitting diagonally across a practice ground leaves you open to a dangerous tendency to restrict the shoulder turn and swing the club out of line on the downswing. Maintenance of the club line is the whole object of the golf swing and to facilitate this you must hit parallel to the defined line of the driving range or practice ground.

Essentially, our practice advice is the same as that we would give to the beginner. It is of the utmost importance when building your swing that you tee the ball up. Whilst learning a new swing, you should give yourself every advantage. Your priority is to groove your swing shape and learn to deliver the clubhead squarely into the back of the ball. As your swing becomes natural and evolves into a free-flowing movement the ball can be moved to the ground with very little difficulty.

Always start your sessions with the shorter clubs. Practise the swing's master key, the backswing hand line, pre-square the blade six inches before impact and take every swing through to a balanced hip height level – the Knightsbridge swing model's DNA.

Hit your first ten to fifteen shots in slow motion to ensure that you are moving through the correct angles. Gradually increase your swing speed until it is about three-quarters of what you believe is your natural tempo. In this way you will replicate the tempo of those at the very top of the game.

One of the most common errors into which your practice can lead you is the temptation to reel off shot after shot in quickfire style. This will unquestionably cause your swing to become quicker and quicker. The swing needs to be smooth and unhurried at all times. Take your time between each shot, and relax for a few minutes between each six or seven.

Never flog yourself into a state of exhaustion. Forcing your limbs and muscles to carry on under the strain of fatigue is sheer misplaced enthusiasm – more harmful than beneficial. Little and often is preferable to driving yourself onto your knees in one prolonged bout. Pack up when you feel the first signs of weariness.

Finally, try to visit a European or Ladies' tour event. Forget the course and following your particular favourite. Instead, take to the practice ground and observe the greats, especially the new generation. You will see how they

LEFT
Notice how the greats go through their practice sessions. They will take the utmost care in perfecting the takeaway to halfway back and check the blade position at the top of the backswing.

go through their routines in exactly the way that we prescribe. They will take the utmost care in perfecting the takeaway to halfway back position and check the blade position at the top of the backswing. Observe their tempo and the balanced finish that they hold until the ball has almost come to rest.

You will also see how they begin their sessions with the short irons and gradually move up through the mid-to-long irons, fairway woods and finally the driver. If they start to struggle with the long clubs, they drop down to the short and mid-irons, until they feel they have got their swing back on track. You, of course, should do the same.

Watching golf on TV is also a great help. Not, we hasten to add, golf instruction – which can be contradictory and confusing. But watching the great players driving and peppering the pin with their irons is most educational. Super slow motion cameras, ball-tracking graphics and interesting camera angles add to the entertainment and more than make up for, in our opinion, far too much airtime being taken up on the putting green!

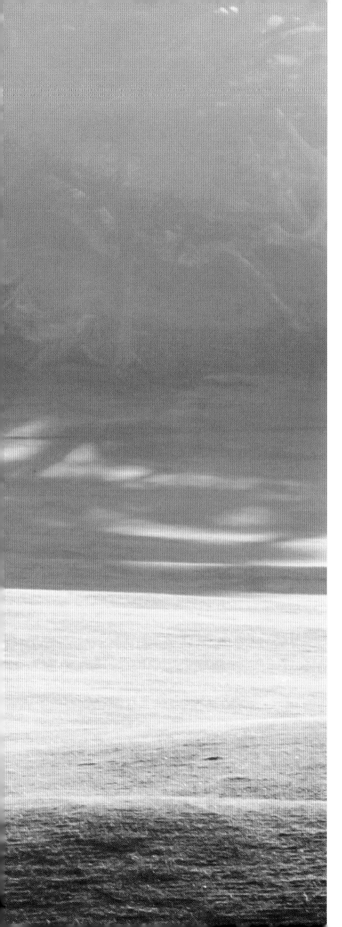

96

Playing with your pro

Playing with your local club pro is an option available to all and something we highly recommend as a great way to improve your golf.

Learning a structured swing is, of course, an essential, but once acquired it is important to learn how to navigate your way around the golf course and deal with its numerous obstacles and challenges. It is also of great value to observe the professional's approach to the game and to copy the beautiful tempo that holds his swing together.

His swing's rhythm is also apparent in his behaviour on the course. He will usually carry his bag, walk purposefully but steadily between shots and approach each shot in a calm, assured manner. In short, his measured tempo will run not only through his swing but throughout his demeanour during the round.

Although not always possible, especially if you are a beginner or high handicapper, it is a great advantage to play with the better player, as their mannerisms will undoubtedly rub off on you. You may have played some of your best golf after watching the Open, the Masters or Ryder Cup contests on TV. Consciously and subconsciously, seeing great players perform under intense pressure with a smooth tempo and faultless basics will undoubtedly stay with you during your next round. So, treat yourself and, if you are financially able to, make your round with the pro a regular monthly event.

97

The golf delusion
is alive and well

As the finishing touches were being put to this book we received a call from a pupil that proved, if proof were needed, that the golf delusion is alive and well and being lived by the majority of amateur golfers.

The call was from a lady who had been highly recommended to us and had booked and paid for three lessons in August 2008. She took her first half-hour lesson in August, the second in October and had, in January 2009, concluded that the lessons weren't working and she would be extremely annoyed if we didn't refund her for her untaken third.

We have been in golf for a very long time and have seen and heard some weird and wonderful theories, but nothing had quite prepared us for the logic of this seriously deluded woman. She did, indeed, have potential but had a high 18 handicap and had, sadly, a very poor swing. Needless to say, the hands and the wrists twisted hideously in the takeaway, the hips were blocked at impact and her finish was no more than an afterthought. Quite frankly, her swing was in a bit of a state and needed a little work. Nothing too drastic, just the basics that we create in all our pupils. This would have only taken a few weeks and was no more than

a routine job. However, she obviously thought that no more than a quick fix was needed and that by simply thinking about it she had cured her rolling wrists and was turning her hips nicely into impact but was still playing dreadful golf. Therefore she concluded that we had wrongly analysed her swing and it was obviously something else that was causing the problem.

By now you should realise that simply thinking about a change won't cure the problem. The swing has to be re-learnt under the strictest possible conditions, in the smallest possible movements and at the slowest possible speed. One piece at a time, bit by bit, stage by stage. It is the only possible way a perennial struggler can progress to a level that they would never have thought possible. It's what we do and what we see our pupils achieve every day of our working lives.

In conclusion, we did refund our lady pupil. It wasn't a lot of money. We charge only slightly more than your club pro, which goes towards paying Knightsbridge rents and business rates. We have no idea what this lady did with her refund, but maybe she put it towards buying yet another set of clubs and pursuing yet another golf delusion…

98

Why we have not franchised

We are often contacted by golfers from all over the world asking whether we have any schools in their particular country or town. Though we would never rule out franchising, we feel strongly that it has to be done properly.

Unfortunately, the bigger things get, the bigger the problems become. A deep working knowledge acquired by many years of one-to-one experience is the only pre-requisite to becoming a successful teacher. Once those with only a basic knowledge of the system are allowed to use it, the more the product's standards will slip, and the brand becomes tarnished.

We have seen this happen to so many other great teachers who have popularised their systems on a worldwide scale. We are constantly visited by pupils who have been to their Academies and spent thousands on lessons and tuition packages, yet they can hardly even make a basic swing shape, and usually have no idea of where the club should be at any point of their swing. They are, in short, totally confused.

Once we have taken them through our swing analysis and shown them how to build a swing shape, they all, without exception, respond by saying, "That is so simple. How come no one else told me that?"

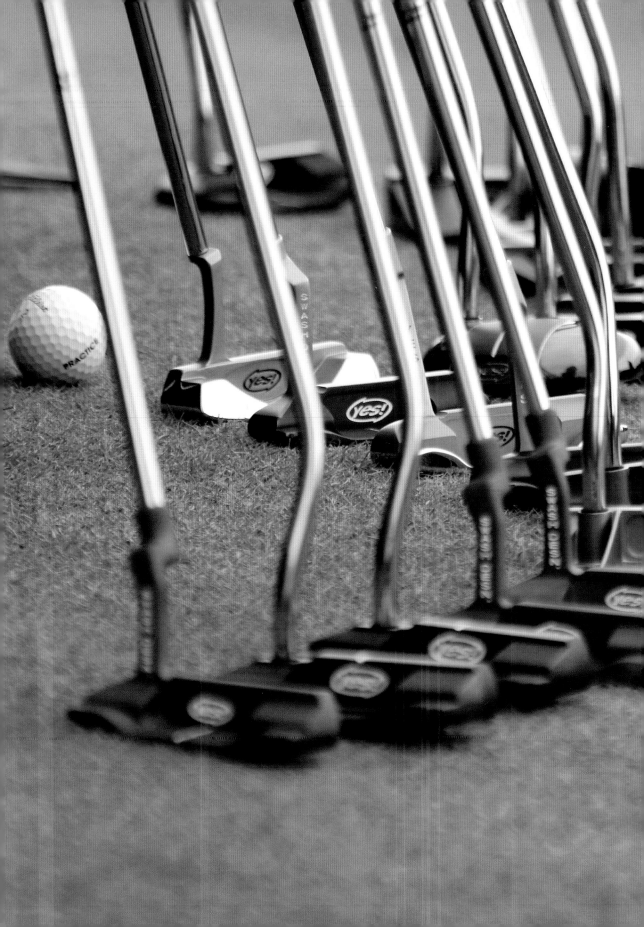

99

More golf delusions

The golf delusion is, of course, the belief that the next quick tip or instant fix will magically transform you from rabbit to Tiger. There are, however, further golf delusions. We've already told you that it is not likely to be your alignment that is at fault, it is almost certainly your swing. We've also explained how the mind is only relevant once you have sorted out the swing's structure and learnt its essential DNA.

Let's first look at a couple of other delusions and begin with the idea that a new set of custom-made golf clubs will perform the miracle that you are so desperately searching for. Good custom-made clubs are certainly a big advantage and something we recommend. But again, as with the mind, only relevant once you have built yourself a sound, modelled swing. Wasting money on clubs that are built to compensate for your swing's deficiencies can only make matters worse and your technique will deteriorate even further.

How about this one? "I can make a great practice swing but when it comes to hitting the ball my swing just falls apart." Well, anyone can hit daisies and the truth is that if there were a ball in the way of your practice swing its flight would once again prove how poor your swing had been. But, in fairness, there is a grain of truth in this. You have read about the dangers of the reflex and how the desire to hit the ball triggers the reflex and destroys the plane of the swing. In the practice swing, of course, there is no ball for the reflex to lunge at. Therefore the swing is smoother, slower and appears to be more in control but, trust us, the wrists are still rolling, the hips are still blocked at impact and the finish is still no more than an afterthought!

100

Vernon Kay

Early pioneers of what we would recognise as golf, Scottish shepherds and fishermen in the middle ages, faced the same challenges from this infuriating game as we all do. Today, millions of people across the globe play golf as an enjoyable pastime, every single one of them trying to fight the demons of their frustrated forebears.

The more the demons win and defeat us, the more we want to go back on the links and prove to them that they can be beaten. It is because of this that, over generations, many a golfing technique has been devised to cast away the twin evils of defeat and humiliation!

Now, as a golfer, you have to trust and believe me when I say I have tried many of these techniques. I've used many tips from magazines and books to overcome the awful feelings those early golfers must have felt which drove them to despair. I have been playing golf for four years now and – finally – I'm happy.

If I'd known then, four years ago, what I have recently learnt from the Knightsbridge Golf School, I swear I would be off scratch leaping with joy.

The easy-to-use, easy-to-follow techniques I've been taught makes the fundamentals of golf easy to understand and control. If you follow the contents of this book, not only will you become a better golfer but you will also be able to understand where you're going wrong. As we all know, when you have a great score on the card going into that tough par four, the last thing you need in your head are the voices of those golfing demons chipping away, telling you your technique isn't good enough to overcome the challenge.

Since meeting the guys at the school I now turn up on the first tee confident that I will play to my handicap or better it. My golf has improved dramatically since using this simple yet effective method. This technique has passed the test of time. Just look at all the pictures in this book and pretty soon your swing will look like Faldo's at the top. Or Tiger's as you release the club into the back of the ball.

In golf we are all looking for the secret of the swing, but believe me there ain't one. The lessons from the Knightsbridge Golf School are the closest you'll get to perfect!

Vernon Kay

101

Leslie King 2009

Leslie King died in 1995. He had enjoyed a lifetime of teaching golf and devising his teaching model. He taught tens of thousands of golfers of all ages and abilities, achieving outstanding results working with no more than the help of his own eyes.

He was outspoken and told it as he saw it. He never told anyone what they wanted to hear just to make them happy. He was his era's equivalent of Brian Clough or José Mourinho, and even after years and years of being a father figure to us, we still addressed him as Mr King. With this in mind you can well understand why he never became the household name he should have been. He simply upset too many people with his honest opinions.

When he was teaching Michael Bonallack, Britain's greatest-ever amateur golfer, the British selectors visited the school and told him that he should be the selected teacher for the Great Britain Team. You could say they were the pompous bunch you might expect. Old school ties, fond of rules and regulations. After listening to them for ten minutes and being told of what they'd expect from him and what an honour it was to be asked, he shook his head, looked them up and down and said "How can you select a team when you don't know anything about golf?"

We've mentioned his egalitarian approach throughout, even to the legendary Henry Cotton, so by now you probably have some idea of the sort of character we are talking about. With this in mind, here are what we believe would be Leslie King's views on modern equipment in the year 2009:

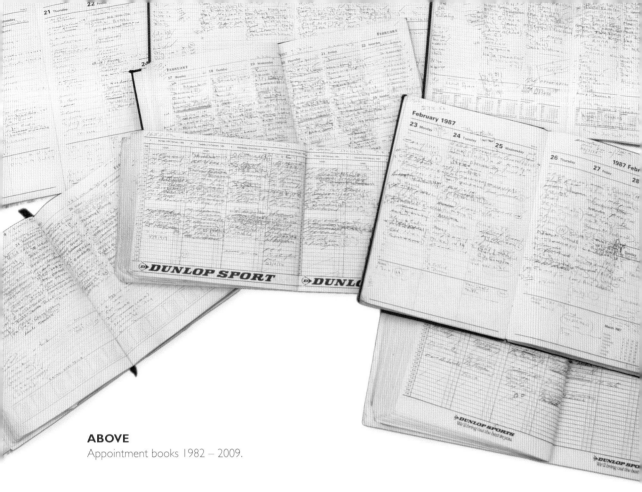

ABOVE
Appointment books 1982 – 2009.

"I am all for the advances in equipment that have made the game so much easier for the average player. Modern clubs are far more forgiving and golfers now hit a greater percentage of good shots. Mishit shots still fly forwards and considerable distance has been added to the average player's drive.

It was very different in my day. There were very few clubs that I found suitable for the average golfer. Most clubs were far too clumsy for my liking. They were heavy. They were badly balanced and the ball had to be struck right out of the middle of the blade for it to move forwards. If a light set were selected, they lacked guts and were more like a wand than a golf club. There were good clubs around but you had to search for them and I would do my best to find them. Interestingly, some old pupils of mine

still visit the school with the clubs I got for them years and years ago. As soon as my boys pick up these old relics, they immediately can tell that I supplied them in my time at the school. Now, as for their use on the tour, well that is something that I feel needs to be discussed. And as every old pro will tell you, you had to be a real shot maker to get the best out of these old-fashioned clubs.

In addition to clubs, the golf ball itself has undergone a big change and once more I am totally in favour of it for the average golfer. But its use on tour is, in my eyes, open for debate."

Of course we can only imagine what our former mentor would have made of today's golfing world. We will keep trying to pass on what he taught us to as many people as we can.

102

Conclusion

The teachings contained within this book have been tried and tested and proven over the last sixty years. At the time of writing we have had a combined experience of teaching golfers of all standards and abilities every half-hour for every working day and month over a seventy-year period.

If the book seems a little dogmatic, we apologise. However, it is our life's work. We have seen teachers come and go, we have seen this and that latest swing discovery, this and that new technique, but none of it has made any difference to the average golfer. The sad fact is that first-time visitors to the school are as bad as they were sixty years ago. In fairness, the general body poise of the swing (i.e. posture at address, backswing, shoulder pitch and turn) are now well understood. But the essential hand line – the most important thing in the golf swing – is still as grey an area as it has always been. Even great players, those blessed with the Hands of God, struggle to keep the club on line throughout the backswing. One minute they are told that they take the club back too far inside. Then they take the club too far outside to compensate and, in so doing, create another series of problems. What even great natural players lack is a total model golf swing: a blueprint for where they should be at each and every stage of their swing. Their phenomenal natural ability has always seen them through and they've only ever needed a tour teacher to tweak their brilliant talent.

For the perennial struggler it is not as straightforward as that. The only way an average player can make a permanent change to the standard of their golf is by learning a shaped, modelled swing that creates the swing's essential DNA and allows the hands to deliver the clubhead squarely, powerfully and consistently into the ball and beyond into the controlled shaped finish.

If, having read this book, you are unsure of any of its teachings, if you don't understand anything that you have read, please do not hesitate to contact us and we will answer your questions. We can be contacted on 0207 235 2468. You will probably get the answerphone that Des Lynam wasn't so keen on but please leave your number and, rest assured, we will get back to you.

In closing, we must once again assure you that almost all golfers on the planet suffer from the faults outlined in this book. Learning the swing stages that comprise the swing's DNA will address these faults and give you a solid, reliable golf swing that will last for life.